For The
LONG TERM

David Coleman

Concept Publishing
York, New York 14592
1979

For The
LONG
TERM

David Coleman

For The Long Term

Library of Congress Catalog Card No. 78-059906

ISBN   Hard: 0-930726-05-7
ISBN   Soft: 0-930726-04-9

Published By
Concept Publishing
Box 203
York, New York 14592

Preface

Capital markets fulfill a distribution function. They bring together the capitalist with the ready supply of money for potentially profitable ventures, and the entrepreneur with the need for captial to fulfill his ideas. That is the way the system should work, and the pretense under which until now it has operated. Unfortunately, the market does not serve that function effectively. An investor cannot make an investment in a venture, relying on the profits of that venture to provide him a good return. Valuation of stock too often is not adequately related to the profitability of the venture. One particular company may sell at a P/E of 20 while another more profitable company will sell at a P/E of 3. That same company that sold at a P/E of 3 today may sell at a P/E of 8 tomorrow.

If you recognize such vagaries of the market, they can work to your advantage most dearly. However, you must then recognize that you are no longer investing; you are speculating with the market, and the basic functioning of the market is no longer being served. This is the kind of market that exists today. There is no market stability, and it is a highly dangerous medium for an unwary investor.

I still recall my consternation about twenty years

ago when I first read of the function of the specialist in the New York Exchange. It said that the specialist smoothed the aberrations of the market by buying stock for his account when the price was high and supply exceeded demand. When demand was strong, he whould sell from his supply to fulfill the numerous orders that could not otherwise be filled. Surely, I reasoned, the function of the specialist would lead to his financial ruin. Yet, the position seemed to be a desirable and rewarding one, and much sought after. The whole thing didn't make sense.

It was some time before my naiveté would allow me to believe the obvious; it is the specialist who controls at least the short term price. Vacillations from specialist actions are even increasing, and with the development of the options market, are becoming excessive for even a short term market. An investor who is searching for a proper capital (long term) market can find little in appropriate investments. There is little true "auction" market in operation on the organized exchanges. Now that the lesson is learned, life is much simpler, and it is no longer necessary to be misled by an approach to investing in the market. It is now possible to "play the market", and study its operation directly.

I am presenting one approach to the market here that has been learned through experience. It is the approach that is recommened to the would-be investor with a desire to make maximum gains with minimum risk. Minimum risk, in this approach, means capital preservation. That is accomplished by reducing downside potential, so that in a worst case, there is no capital loss. On the other extreme, upside potential is expanded so that potential return from capital appreciation promises high reward. Thus, while preserving capital and protecting his investments from the actions of the market, the investor can allow the market to serve his investment objectives.

More simply, through this approach, it is possible to use what has become a controlled and overly liquid short term money market for the purposes of **long term** capital investing.

David Coleman

Credits

As he has done for me on other publications, Professor Mark Price, College of General Studies, Rochester Institute of Technology added greatly to the clarity of this book. He provided a moderation to my technical bent, by keeping in mind constantly the audience for whom this book is intended. A reorganization of the parts and chapters should significantly improve understanding by the reader.

Detailed review and improvements by Professor Price to my often abrupt style of presentation should allow the reader to more succinctly follow the important ideas being developed, and to better appreciate the background from which the ideas were developed.

Any remaining errors are mine, of course.

Figure 6-2. Stock Market Cycles is reproduced from a book by John Sullivan, *How To Beat The Stock Market Rip-Off*, published by Hawkes Publishing Inc., Salt Lake City, Utah, 1976, and used with permission of the author.

Cover design, type composition and graphics are by J.J.Phillips, Inc., Rochester, New York
Printing and binding is by Rochester Business Services, Inc., Rochester, New York

Contents

A look at methods of the future for profitability now.
Vacillation...value to individual...mean and variance...the third moment ...Beta...probability profile...business and market risk...time...market segments...bias...conceptual view...detailed analysis...risk minimization.

Bulls and bears can make money, pigs rarely do.
Risk/return relation...business risk and market risk...financial risk...when to sell...average return...market segments...buy and sell timing ...portfolios...levels of growth...potential returns.

Physical proximity...proximity through knowledge...financial risk (Balance Sheet)...business risk (P&L)...market risk (price)...risk minimization...timing: market moods, market segments, overreactions...personal goals.

List of Figures

List of Tables

Introduction

In any economic endeavor, it is necessary to have a long range goal to maintain advancement toward that objective. Without such a goal, individual actions are poorly directed, and the direction may vary from moving toward that objective. With a proper goal, mistakes will be made that cause minor vacillations in direction, but each error tends to reinforce the learning and understanding needed to maintain a straighter course.

It's not much different in investing. If an investor sets realistic goals and sets them high enough to sustain his objectives over a considerable length of time, each move in the market and within the portfolio will reinforce his ability to pursue those goals. What is considered within the scope of the long range plan is the conceptual understanding of the market and its moods, in relation to the needs and wishes of the individual investor. It is not possible to tell each investor what is best for him; that he must decide for himself. It is possible to point to some possibilities in the market to help the investor determine reasonable goals.

The need of the particular investor is probably a need to invest capital, to maintain it and profit from it over time. By investing is meant the assumption of a business risk for gain through the use of capital. It will not come as much of a surprise to the experienced investors to be told that the market is not for investing. Certainly, an investor can buy fixed income securities in the market that will yield a return somewhat above inflation. But caught in the wrong end of the interest rate fluctuations, the investor could emerge from such an investment with a highly depreciated capital account. Thus, in addition to business risk the investor must face financial risk arising from the money medium in which capital is held.

An investor can certainly purchase securities in a thriving business that pays reasonable dividends and has the capacity to grow, often from internally generated capital. But the investor will find that the market is not a direct reflection of the economic situation, and an increase in dividends often is received by the market in conjunction with a price decrease. As a minimum, a stock selling for a 25 price/earnings ratio (P/E) today may sell for an 18 P/E tomorrow. Thus, in addition to business risk and financial risk, a third risk, the market risk is added to the perils of the investor. When that risk reaches excessive levels, as it has in today's market, the act of investing becomes highly speculative.

Of course, the investor could accept smaller returns for a refusal to risk capital, and maintain short term returns that would be reasonably safe. Inflation would eat away at capital over time, but by this method of living on capital, the investments could be safe from the variances of the market. But these variances should not so easily be pronounced as undesirable. They are a reflection of a dynamic business scene that is capable of yielding exceptional returns to all members of the economic system. It is a symptom of the fervor that built our country, supported its social institutions, and helped develop the capital that is available for investing.

Therefore, it is necessary to resolve to protect that capital from those factors that might wield control over portions of the market, recognize that variances exist, and work to understand how to use these fluctuations to an advantage. What should be recognized is that the market will not support investors who merely want their capital to work for them. The assumption of such large risk is speculation, and objectives must be explicitly stated to reflect this recognition.

This does not mean that an investor must subject his capital to the market risk, and hope the variances will serve his objectives. Careful speculation can be controlled, and potential variations are not risky if they work for the investor, adding to the value of an investment that he holds.

Speculation might entail the purchasing of a security that yields no direct return (dividend), and no promise of future return. In such a risk situation, the potential yields (capital gains) must be very high. The same is true for any purchase that is made with the understanding that returns are speculative. If the investor could keep the high returns and at least diminish the risk, the market could be made to respond to his investment objectives over time with a most handsome reward.

That is the entire purpose: to look at ways to minimize the risk of the market. The method presented here will concentrate on minimizing the downside risk, while accepting the appreciation of investments. The market promises return in exchange for risk (or variability). An effective speculator accepts upward risk and minimizes loss.

There are many techniques that will help to accomplish this goal. What is presented here should allow the investor to pursue this goal with renewed understanding and direction. It is necessary to feel the mood of the market in the long run. In the 60's, the market ran wild with mounting P/E's sometimes substantiated by very little solid economic base. In the 70's, there is a return to fundamental values, and a resulting long term bear market. The market will overadjust, as it always does, and the early 80's will bring more reasonable values in the market, provided inflation can be moderated.

Within the flow of those moods, a business cycle beats its way, as it has for as long as records have been kept. The market shows the way of this cycle, leading it by about six months. In recent years, since WW II, the fluctuations of the business cycle have become even more severe, with government intervention to "stop the cycle". It is not always possible to control economic reactions with public controls, as the government has tried to do. We are made to think that economic agents, such as businessmen have responses cast in concrete, and what they did last cycle they will repeat without concern for governmental actions. Of course, the cycle deepens. Little by little, we are learning that incentives and not controls will change the cyclical responses for the better. At that point there will be a lengthening of the cycle time period, and a dampening of its fluctuations.

Within the market itself, there are different responses from different types of investors. There are risk averters, those who try to hide from the variances of the market, rather than use them to their advantage. These conservative souls impose an important stability to the market, and are an important segment of the market in measuring its depth. Their characteristics are different from other segments of the market, in that they are the true investors who merely want their capital to work for them. Unfortunately, their segment of the market can be even more volatile than that of the speculators.

In the middle of the market (the central market) is a segment that dominates in setting the mood of the market. There is almost a mathematical relation to their acceptance of risk in relation to a return on their investment. They set prices in the market to the tune of this relation.

At the other end of the market from the risk averters are the speculators, who will take a chance on anything, as long as the potential return has been priced high enough. At the extreme, this segment of the market is the vulture who will clean up the throw-aways of the central market. The overall price for these services is extremely reasonable, with these investors usually receiving less overall return on the average than the central market, even though exceptional risk is assumed. It takes a true gambler's spirit to participate at this end of the market.

No effective investor stays within a particular segment of the market throughout its ups and downs. He continually searches for better buys, and shifts from one type of investment to another in seeking to fulfill his goals. As the market gains confidence in economic events, he searches for better returns, and delves deeper into the market's depth, assuming more risk in a particular security, when he feels that the risk is lessened by the general trend of the market. Anticipation of this deepening of the market can further lessen his risk, and such speculation can pay well. A general market rise does not happen across the board. It grows throughout the market over a period of time, as the depths of the market are searched for better return.

As the trends of the market are pulled by economic events, investors will switch among different types of investments. In good times or in anticipation of them, the investor seeks stocks in industrials. When a downturn is anticipated by the market, investors seek more stable returns, and shift to fixed income stocks and securities. This move is accelerated by the shifting interest rate cycle, and the effective speculator can again be well rewarded. In real estate investment, the three rules are usually given as, "location, location, and location". In the general capital markets, the three rules are, "timing, timing, and timing".

What I have given here are methods of anticipating the flows of the market so that adequate returns can be maintained while minimizing the attendant risk. While it must be labeled speculation (since appreciation plays an important part in maintaining adequate returns), it is not for speculators alone. It is a requirement for the survival of any investor to understand the vacillations of the market and use them to his advantage, in order to fulfill his long range investment goals.

Part I

The Character of the Market

For The Long Term

The long term investor makes his investment in a capital market. This market is a long term market that serves the purpose of bringing together the investor and the entrepreneur. If a proper association can be found, that is, if the investor can find an appropriate price, they both can profit from well laid business plans and effective execution.

But that price that the investor so carefully evaluated is not a long range consideration in the real market. The market character is not long range as its purpose would require. The market prices are constantly moving, even though the values of the underlying securities are not changing. These movements without underlying values typically carry the market prices to extremes from which it must then retreat. The excesses of price movement always require a correction over time.

Thus, the investor not only must accept the business risk inherent in a capitalist venture (an assumable risk), and absorb the financial risk inherent in a financial market (an acceptable risk), but he must deal with a market risk of valuation in time, whose volatility makes that risk unacceptable. The lack of reflection of values in prices is not an adequate character for a long term capital market, and the market becomes unsuitable for investing.

However, it is still possible for the investor to participate in the market. Recognizing the characteristics of the market can reduce the risk associated with them, and it is entirely possible to use these characteristics to the advantage of the investor. That market risk still must be assumed, and an overt recognition must be made that investment objectives can only be obtained by limiting that risk to acceptable proportions, or turning it to the advantage of the investor. It is possible to do that, reducing the speculative character of the market so that an investor can attain his investment objectives.

The Dow Jones Industrial Average, adjusted for inflation by the Consumer Price Index, is now at almost the level where it stood in 1927.* This was just prior to the runup to overpricing that led to the crash of '29. In other words, in the last fifty years, the Dow hasn't gained in value. All those profits that were ploughed back have produced new profits only adequate to discount inflation. During that period, it was the individual investors who compiled the best record. They outperformed the institutional investors and profited from the market. The individual investor can make money in the market and he can do so consistently. To do this, he must understand the characteristics of the market and allow them to work for him.

If the characteristics of the market are somewhat consistent, and subject to some degree of control by the investor, why is it that many professional investors so consistently underperform the market averages? It is a fascinating side of the failure of the market to fulfill its purposes. The money managers have never had an objective to make money for the investors: their objective has always been to sell additional shares of the fund. That is not to say that investors pursue the wrong objectives. For the most part, the individual investor is insulated from the money manager, often through law requiring institutional "control" of money funds such as pensions.

The investor will find in this Part a side of the market not often understood and less often presented in the financial press. It is a side of the market that must be used effectively for successful investing.

---

* *The M/G Financial Weekly Market Digest,* Media General Financial Services Inc., Richmond, VA updates their "Constant-Dollar Dow" monthly, and frequently prints the long term chart.

Chapter 1

Overreaction

The human frailty that rules the market

The market appears to have one prominent characteristic: it is constantly moving. If it is not going up, then it is going down. It is unstable, and this constant movement seems to be inherent to its operation. It often does not seem possible to filter out the constant change, and to approach the market for a capital investment. No real investment is possible, for the changing character of the market always dominates.

The adjustment process should be expected in an open auction market, but in an auction a buyer and seller determine a common price, and strike a bargain. In the market, no final price is ever struck, and yesterday's value is erroneous for today. If an antique eighteenth century chest is sold at auction for $20,000, that auction price becomes a reasonable measure, as a base, of what the value will be in the future. If, on the other hand, a stock is purchased at a P/E of 8 (a reasonable long term value), the future value might be at a P/E of 5. The stock hasn't changed. The earnings flow might be quite stable, but the value is different because the "market is down".

Fads and fashion are always part of an auction, and the general level of optimism is always part of an open market. But even at its lowest, an auction over a reasonable time period will usually recognize intrinsic value. The stock market is at times incapable of doing this. It is, in fact, not an auction market. At one extreme it is controlled, and at the other it runs strictly on emotion. Neither provides an adequate base in itself for a strong capital market. A true capital market is of a long term character, and the stability for that character to develop in the stock market is not present. It is an institution that has forgotten its purpose, to provide entrepreneural capital, and is only fulfilling it in at least a flawed fashion. The market overreacts up as well as down so that capital appreciation is possible, but the risk that must be assumed is unacceptable to investors.

It would appear that we don't have a very good hold on valuation techniques. If a stock can vacillate by so wide a margin in price, then we must not know what the true or correct price really is. Actually, quite the contrary is true. A reasonable return can be computed quickly, within some measurable limits of accuracy. The long term return on capital is approximately 3%, and to this must be added compensation for inflation, and a risk premium. While there is not too much legitimate base for the risk premium in financial theory today, the market usually has it pegged within a small range. The total required return should establish the correct price within quite a small margin, if the stock potential is viewed over the long term.

Why then don't we simply establish a range of value, and allow the stock issue to trade within that small margin? There must be something that causes the basic instability of the market. In fact, there are factors both internal and external to the market that are constant sources of irritation, propelling the market one way or another, and causing maladjustments that force the market away from what might have been a basic equilibrium. Here we want to look at some of the internal factors that preclude a natural stability in the market. In Chapter 3, we will consider some of the external factors.

The very construct of the market is one of the major causes of its instability. The participants consist of many smaller organizations and individuals, so that no one participant has a strong effect on the direction of the market. There is no large leadership in the market. At any one particular time, it is even difficult to get agreement on where the market stands or in what direction it might be heading. This lack of leadership subjects the market to highly variable impetus so that uncertainty exists to some degree on the part of all participants. The need to overcome this uncertainty causes the rushing movements of the market that frequently overshoot their objective. A movement may be slow in developing, but once underway, it has great strength, and is difficult to stop.

In this way, the market is much like the housing industry. The housing industry is made up of many small builders and contractors, and no one company or group has a measurable effect on the direction of activity. The industry is slow to move, usually lagging the business cycle on both its up and down movements. Once it is prodded into action, its moves are strong, being much more volatile than the business cycle. The upswing usually is longer than the business cycle, and the declines are crashes. In good times of available money for real estate, builders typically put their crews to work with little adequate long range planning, or understanding of housing demand. The result is an overbuilding that usually leaves builders with an inventory at a time when no funds are available to finance the finished construction. Apartments and commercial structures stand vacant, and profits drop drastically. With builder financing very expensive, and take-out financing nonexistent, builders stop building, until demand can overtake the existing supply of structures. Again the builders are slow to act, and completed real estate comes into short supply once more. The process begins again, but never adjusts to an equilibrium. **13**

The market is like that, in overreacting to the stimuli of the perception of future events. If it sees tighter money coming, with higher interest rates, it will begin to discount stock prices so that they yield an adequate return. But then the market is going down, so that the investor faces the uncertainty of an adequate rate of return in addition to a declining market. The market is double counting a single event, but the pervasiveness of a mood in the market perpetuates itself. There is no leader to tell the market to stop, and so it continues beyond its original goal of discounting prices to a reasonable return. It may have been slow to begin the move, but once in motion, its inertia carries it beyond the point of reasonable adjustment.

It is a statistical process. Populations composed of numerous small entities tend to overreact to a stimulus. They are slow to begin action, so that the stimulus must be strong. Thus, the reaction to that stimulus will be strong. Once in motion, the movement obtains an inertia that will typically carry it beyond the point of normal equilibrium. In some systems, as is sometimes true in the market, the necessity of reacting to the overreaction can become an adequate impetus to start movement in the other direction. Given adequate generation internally, the system can become self-generative of its oscillations. Without external damping, there is no normal equilibrium.

Knowledge is the best damping device in any system. If the participants act through calculated planning, most selfgenerative systems begin to quiet, and the oscillations become longer in time as they decline in amplitude. In housing, the factory built house, and other similar cost cutting measures recently developed, may have the effect of consolidating the industry to some degree. The result will be more capable personnel leading the industry, and a more concentrated opinion of possible events. The industry could find itself less generative of overreaction and the attendant oscillations.

In the market, one might initially think that the use of

computers in reviewing the market would bring about better adjustment. They probably bring about a more efficient market by quicker adjustment to a particular level. But they are of little use in determining at what level the market will operate. However, the market is smarter today than yesterday, and we are slowly learning more about the operation of the market, the valuation techniques, and the requirements for efficiency. There is statistical evidence that the market lead of the business cycle has decreased, indicating less reliance on speculation and more direct contact with the economics facts as they unfold. Some damping of the oscillations of the market cycle has not yet appeared, though. One development that is likely to deter the damping of the market cycle is negotiated rates. Where once basic research was underwritten by a portion of broker rates, now it appears that fewer and fewer analysts will be reviewing the market. It should have little effect on the major issues, but the efficiency of the market in depth must surely be effected detrimentally. If you must be mercenary, yes, that poses opportunities for the alert investor, but that efficient market is needed when it is time to sell. The lack of sufficient depth can only deter the maturing of the market, to the detriment of all.

Of course, the market is still under emotional control. The numbers and facts have little to do with stock prices. It is possible to be completely right in assessing the business risk, and still fall prey to the financial risk. Effective investing must be through a disciplined approach that recognizes the character of the market (medium) as well as the specific security (vehicle). Most security analysts overestimate earnings and price potential at the peak, and underestimate them at the bottom. Certainly, there is a reluctance to endorse anything controversial at the bottom, when investor pessimism is high. It evidently is felt that it is better to tell the investors what they want to hear, than to consider upsetting everything with a more valid analysis. There seems to be little positive feedback from the investors to the analysts. That is probably more to the detriment of the analysts. If they don't know how bad they are, they can't improve, and if they don't improve, the market will continue to vacillate in its self-generative cycles. It might be assumed that the analysts would police themselves, but human nature being what it is, poor performance can be easily forgotten, or dismissed as the result of uncontrollable and nonrecurring factors.

That kind of market operation is ideal for the conceptualist who is strong enough to read the signs, and follow predefined plans toward whatever goals are desired from the market. The ability to anticipate economic events often lies with horse sense and experience, as strongly as with technical expertise. The typical lag in govenmental decision-making more often than not interferes with economic operation rather than helping it, and reinforces the business cycle, rather than damping it as intended. The average American can look down the road and see that a $100 billion deficit will add to the inflation rate. The effect on the capital markets is obvious, and profitable for the investor strong enough to stick with some long range convictions.

Of course, there is a lack of long range data. Institutions are constantly changing, and each few years brings changes in the important formative events underlying economic developments. Not all changes are to the good. A capital market serves the purpose of providing long range funds for business operation. The stock market has no long range goals as an institution, nor has it effectively operating long range characteristics. The stock market is today operating as a money market fund, providing only short term stability to both sides of the exchange of capital. That unfortunate circumstance doesn't appear likely to change at least in the near term.

A market might be set in an upward motion by numerous things. There is the reaction to the overreaction that is the pepetuating force, but there is also the scrambling

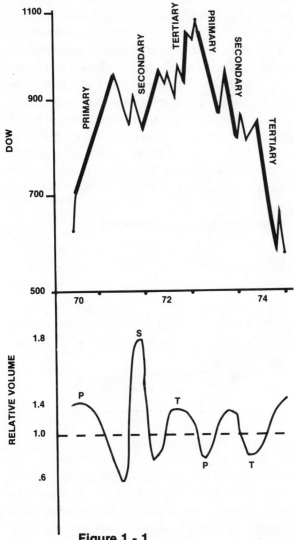

Figure 1 - 1
VOLUME RELATIVE TO MARKET SEGMENTS

to cover the short interest that resulted from the pessimism of a low. That can indeed be strong impetus in today's market of large block trades. In the upswing, it is interesting to note that maximum volume is typically reached at about the midpoint, not at the extremes, or the turning points of the market cycle. A typical volume, picture, is shown in Figure 1-1. There is a long, but moderate peak in volume that is required to begin propelling the market upward, particularly through the primary stocks. At the approximate midpoint of the upward market, there is a break, and the strongest volume occurs to get the market going again. At the end, there is a small rise of volume that forms the final phase of the market, acting primarily on the tertiary stocks.

Figure 1 - 2
TYPICAL REVERSALS IN AN UPTREND

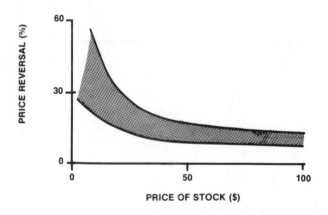

The typical reversals that occur in prices during the breaks of the rise may be of interest. They are shown in Figure 1-2. This is, at best, a rough picture, but the statistical consistency is quite high. Price adjustments are typically small, but with effective technical analysis, the moves can be adequate for good profitability with shorting. Note that the largest percentage moves are usually in the lower priced stocks. These are typically the more volatile stocks, and this effect would be expected. On the downward movement of the cycle, no such consistency has been perceived in the reversals. These moves are subject to high volatility, and carry excessive risk in terms of the rewards for trading. For the average investor, the use of these reversals on the upswing should be limited to upward price movements, without incurring excessive risk. It is difficult to know at what point an upward movement will run out of steam, because of the tendency of the market to overreact. There is thus no fundamental or technical base on which to estimate a relative high except historical data and the general strength of the market. The reversals are of value, though, in determining at what point to enter the market after one of these adjustments. They are also some indication of the changing depth of the market, with a major move beginning toward secondary stocks.

The level of emotion in the market is itself some indication of the level of development of a major market movement. When everyone is thinking along the same line, the trend is nearing an end, for it has been overdone. In the market, a diversity of opinion is always the most healthy situation. "Playing the market", rather than investing in an economic base will tend to increase the amplitude and speed of market fluctuations. We did that in the '60's, but now it is time for the market to mature toward its long term responsibilities of a capital market. The data shows that there is a decreasing lead of the economy by the market. This indicates a more direct reliance on the economic situation, rather than advance speculation, and is a healthy move. There is also a decreasing lead by volume over the general directional movement of the market. It supports the indication of a move toward market stability.

Working against this healthy trend is a high level of political uncertainty, resting primarily on the fiscal irresponsibility that is one of the major causes of an increasingly permanent level of inflation. The market is uncertain if this will remain, and if so, what adjustments to economic structure it will cause. Certainly, these adjustments will be highly disruptive, and require major redistributions in the economy. The uncertainty is shown in Figure 1-3, by the inverted declining coil (or triangle) that has formed over more than the last decade. There are increasing fluctuations in the market from emotional uneasiness while the basic structure of the market is tending toward better stability. Over the long term, we must align ourselves on the side of the change toward structural stability, but the current disruptions in the monetary base of the market have the capacity to destroy it as an effective capital market. Major structural changes in established institutions can come about through slow development, or through immediate, and usually violently disruptive change. We require a stable monetary system for the required changes in the market to be accomplished through slow development.

The trend in the long term is toward increasing understanding of the overreactions of the market. If this understanding is concentrated on market action for profitability, as it will be in the short run, increased vaccillations will result. The actions of the traders will accentuate the general emotional characteristics of the market. It could become severe enough to cause major maladjustments in the market, but I doubt that it is long lived enough to destroy the trading function. In the long term, this understanding will force changes in the structure of the market itself, leading to increased stability. At the current time, the market appears headed toward a base of fundamental value. It seems doubtful that it is true economic acumen, but rather fear and uncertainty that is the motivating force. In the long run, maturity in the ability to function effectively may allow the market to settle toward reasonable values and toward a structural improvement in capital markets. The market may become a place for investing, without the limitations in character which we must now face.

Figure 1 - 3
INCREASING UNCERTAINTY IN THE MARKET

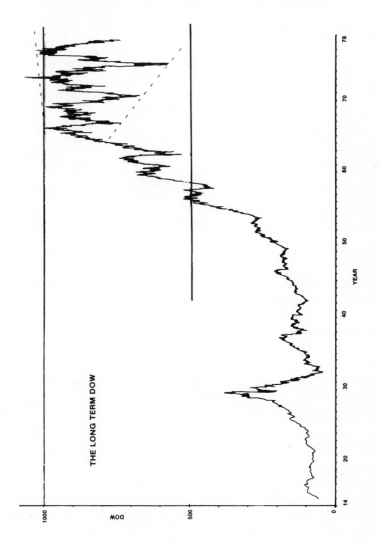

Part I / The Character of the Market

Chapter 2

Not For Investing

*Excess liquidity precludes serving
the needs of the investors.*

The drive for liquidity in the capital markets is a noble effort. It allows the investor to enter the market with funds that would not otherwise be used for that purpose, funds of a shorter term nature than would typically be used in capital markets. The flow of funds into and out of the capital markets are in themselves an indication of how far the necessity for liquidity has been exceeded. The capital markets are by nature long term. It is not possible to decide today to buy that new machine, and tomorrow decide to reverse the decision. Businesses require their capital over the long term, and an investment in business equity should be made with that perspective. An investor should be able to purchase an equity position in a firm at some reasonable value, one that provides a reasonable return, hold that investment over some period of time, and sell it at some value that reflects the operation of the firm over that period.

Today's capital markets have lost the objective of serving as a transit point for capital flowing to business. They have lost their long term nature, and are inundated by short term flows of funds that are disruptive to the functioning of the market, and reduce the time horizon of its objectives. We have seen the excessive speculation in the market that has resulted, but it appears to have reached a peak. We are seeing increased vacillations in the market over the recent near term, but they seem to be the result of uncertainty more than speculation. One is passive while the other is overt, and the strong directional moves toward specific objectives have softened in many of the individual issues that lead the market. The flow of short term money market funds has reversed, into a net outlfow from the capital market, and the inflow of less speculative funds (normally invested in bonds and long term debentures) has reversed also. The extremes of the market, the dominion of the risk averter and the risk taker, are shrinking, and that adds stability to the central market. The movement is slow, and attitudes on the Street often have failed to change with the changing flows of funds. There is typically a time lag from the initiation of tangible events to conception, but the changing attitudes will accelerate the trend, probably by the mid-80's.

The level of return available in the money markets has caught up with our post war inflation, and much of the speculative funds in these markets now support commercial paper, CDs, and other short term instruments. The investment (mutual) funds have been burned badly in the stock market, and their aggressive behavior has turned more passive, so that they are returning to a more conservative stance in their investments. With rising inflation, the public will demand more current income, and this will reinforce the move to income producing investments, even at the sacrifice of the more speculative capital gains. With generally reduced flows of funds into the market, it is likely over the long term to settle to more fundamental values, and the vacillations of the past will quiet into a more normal sinuous rhythm. By the mid-80's we should see a return of value to the capital markets, so that they will more directly provide their proper function of a channel for capital.

24

A capital market, such as the stock market, is for the purpose of investing. By investing is meant the assumption of a business risk within the function of providing capital. An investor provides the funds for a capital asset, such as a piece of equipment, confident that the machine can produce a product at a profit. The bargain between the capitalist and the entrepreneur (often the same person) is typically a long term contract, for it may take years for the machine to pay for itself. The capitalist and entrepreneur profit through productivity and service. The contract is typical of economic activity, such as the contract between the entrepreneur and labor in which both parties are better off following execution. All parties gain, including the ultimate consumer. Speculation is quite different, in that it is a transfer function, in which no material gain is made. It may serve the financial functioning of the market, but is typically short term in nature, and not directly productive, in an economic sense. Speculation is the acceptance of the (short term) financial risk, while investing is acceptance of the (long term) business risk.

The effect of speculation in the market is mostly to change the level of the market. One theory about the market's operation is that it is an efficient market, reflecting most events prior to their occurance. But if we look at the price moves of stocks following public reports of changes in earnings, it is found that about half of a move in price occurs after the announcement.* The moves in general are not adequate to provide a profitable opportunity for the average investor. A trader with low transfer cost and good knowledge of a particular issue might be able to use the information to profit. It might also be that an individual investor could profit from a particularly volatile issue, using

---

*For example, see Stewart L. Brown, "Earnings Changes, Stock Prices, and Market Efficiency", *The Journal of Finance, March 1978* The American Finance Association, New York.

a discount brokerage house to reduce transfer costs. The margin is small and the risk can be high, and that's always a bad investment. It seems the market is only efficient enough to choke off the profitable opportunities, and that is what we would expect. In the market, the average investor is not likely to find the plums lying around. In a stable market, price is always a function of supply and demand, but the short run is controlled by the vacillations and corrections of a functioning market. The long run required to obtain an equilibrium might be longer than a decade, given the disruptive flows of funds that we have seen in the '60s. It is merely a changing mood of the market, but it is controlled, as always, by the fundamental and technical characteristics underlying the market, in the long run.

In the market, it is impossible for anyone to consistently pick the winners. If the professionals of the Street were asked to pick the 100 best performing stocks, the result would be an accuracy of less than 50%. Combine multiple periods, and the results would be astoundingly low. In fact, pure luck or genius can seldom sustain a 10% annual return. At 10%, money doubles approximately every 7 years, and a man of 40 who invested $10,000 could retire with close to a quarter of a million dollars. The world would not permit such nonsense, on the average, but a conservative approach to the market can yield consistent gains while protecting the capital base, so that the investment continues to grow over time. The rate may slow or speed up, but consistency will always provide the best overall return, on the average. The market has never adequately compensated its own extremes. Investors in these market sectors provide an important functioning of the market, but the risk averter by definition is willing to accept a reduced return for a supposed stability. He has always been given the lower return, but the stability has never been achieved. In the extremes of the money market today, the risk averter receives a guaranteed return in governments, but accepts a return less than the inflation rate, so that he is in fact losing capital. That is hardly a riskless position. In the risk taker market, the efficiency of the market is obvious. The stocks that they have shunted to the lower end of the market seldom perform adequately, and enough fail in performance and operation that the overall return to this investor class is below that in the central market. Some of the risk takers profit, and handsomely, but only at the expense of the other risk takers. It is a redistribution mostly within that sector, and such a game is not fitting for someone interested in a capital market.

The favorite game to play in the market is the one that effects the level of the entire market. It is the creation of what has been called Supermoney.* It is capital values based on an earnings flow, and in spite of the publicity gimmick of attaching a buzz-word name to it, it is the basis of all capital values, as it always has been. The only question is the capitalization rate. In the '60s, the market might lie at an average P/E of about 15. That means a return of less than 7%. There may have been some growth stocks that possessed opportunities for capital investments that justified that price. Surely, the market as a whole did not. Today the market lies at about a P/E of 8, half that of the '60s. The result of that price drop is that after sixteen years '62 to '78, the market price level, deflated by the wholesale price index, is unchanged, as measured by the Dow. The 13% return of today contains an inflation premium of 6%, so that even the return level has not changed drastically. The level of the market appears to have changed, but perhaps it has not. It would still be a genius who could have maintained a consistent return over that period.

Much of the problem with finding the level of capitalized earnings comes from the quality of the earnings. The accountants assure us that the statements were prepared

---

*Adam Smith, *Supermoney,* Random House, New York, 1972.

under generally accepted accounting standards (GAAP), but the statement and the procedures that acompany it are routine, and routine procedures are inadequate to warn of changing characteristics, changing management tactics, or fraud. Often time the accountants are aware of significant facts and don't report them. Their fees, after all, come from the managements on whom they are reporting. Discretion often overrules prudence. The supposedly self-governing AICPA is obviously incapable (or unwilling) to perform a fully effective policing function. There is some disagreement among participants as to whether management has the prerogative to report anything but "true" earnings. A capable management might recognize a particularly good year in earnings, while recognizing that the following will be less profitable. It is a question whether they have the right to level out the earnings over time. For the most part, professional investors consider it a proper function of management. They are aware that it can't be hidden, only hidden from view. It is merely a transfer from the P&L to the Balance Sheet, and the professionals will know that it is there. It is typically the individual investors (who probably never read a 10K report), regulators, and outsiders who insist the practice is inappropriate. It is possible for a fraudulent management to throw excess funds in the reserves, reduce earnings, allow the price to drop, and set about acquiring treasury stock. The concern of those opposed to management manipulation is where the line can be drawn between a proper function of management in evaluating the Balance Sheet, and pursuit of a fraud on the market. If it were an efficient market, there would be no need for concern. The market is simply no more perfect than most other man made institutions.

It might be expected that the individual investor would fail to adequately study a potential investment. What is surprising is that every recent case of major fraud has occurred seemingly without a knowledge of it on the part of the directors, or at least a majority of them. Few directors are adequately compensated for the large responsibilities that they assume, and few are adequately qualified for the controlling function that should be theirs. A big name or big title on the board of directors is not an adequate sign that the investor can relax his vigilance. As a negative indicator, it may even signal that the purpose of that director holding the position is for the big name or title only, without any regard to his competence.

The study of fundamentals is always important, but in today's market the vacillations around a reasonable value are primarily market functions. It often seems that the market cycles have become so short and quick that the first investor to panic will be the one with the Rolls. Some of the market movements make it appear that greed alone is the prime motive power in the market. In fact, it is only a symptom of the large inflows of short term funds that have temporarily changed the characteristics of the market. These symptoms will disappear in the long run, but they are with us for at least the next five years.

There is evidence that certain fringe operators have used the excessive swings to perpetrate their own opportunities. One case going to court charges stock manipulation through a major financial newspaper. Whatever the truth of the allegations, the existence of the case will serve notice on the market that a degree of prudence lost in earlier markets should return to investing decisions. It is always healthy for the market to be reminded of the need for fundamental valuation as a prelude to any investment decision.

The specialists, at the core of the market, have not been without their detractors.* There are evidences of price moves completely unsupported by a general market desire to buy or sell. There is one recurring market move that happens at

---

*Richard Ney, *The Wall Street Jungle,* Grove Press, New York, 1970 is one who attempts to understand the market without resorting to an "expose".

Figure 2 - 1
SHAKING THE TREE

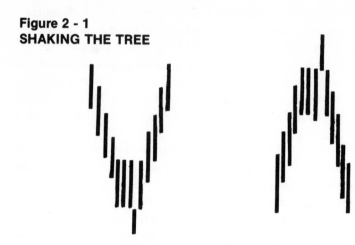

TROUGH   PEAK

least with the participation of the specialist that can be of value to the individual investor. It does not happen in all stocks, but where it appears, it seems to be a regular occurance. As the issue prices run up (down), there will be a temporary lull in the buying (selling), bids are pulled down (up), and selling (buying) will hit the market. What happens, whether manipulated or not, is that a specialist must often sell short on a quick upswing of the market. These shorts are covered on an adjustment (reversal) from the runup. Where this kind of move can be of value is at the peak or trough. The general form of these reversals is shown in Figure 2-1. In the trough, after a bear move, the stock will stabilize within a small range, gaining momentum for a strong bull move. Prior to that move, a lull in the market may be used to drop the bids temporarily, to afford a buying opportunity. Say a stock once at 60 has declined to just above 40, where there appears to be a floor of support. Supported by a general market move, the stock appears to be forming the base for a strong bull move. It would not be surprising to see certain stocks break through that support level in a one day move, with the price dropping to as low as 36 to 38. An investor, aware that the stock may act this way would place an order at something like 38 ½. The period of the trough might be as long as three months or longer, but the five percent premium may be worth the wait. The form at the peak is reflective of the action in the trough. Incidentally, that kind of action, a forced reversal, is called "shaking the tree" (pulling the bids down) so that the baskets can be filled (covering the short sales at a profit). It's not new to the market, but it can be a profitable one to the investor, without risk.

A move that is new to the market is the excessive use of options by traders and specialists. The '77-'78 bear market is the first such market in which a developed options market has been in existence. Many market observers are convinced that it was specialist and market maker trading in those options that contributed most to the record 66.37 million share volume on August 3, 1978. The action starts with a large short interest position and short interest in naked options. (A naked option is the sale of an option when the seller doesn't own the underlying stock. He is betting the stock will decline and it can then be purchased at a lower price.) The market maker knows who holds the short interest and the naked options, information not available to the rest of the market. He buys options on a certain number of shares, and also buys a similar number of shares (long). Now the sham volume begins. The market maker exercises his options (calls) so that investors are forced to buy shares at the market. In a particular stock, a volume of around 100,000 (NYSE) might be enough to force the price up. The market maker now sells his shares at the higher price. This sends the price down where new stock and options can be purchased, and the action is repeated. In a short period such as a bear market reversal, 100,000 shares can easily be churned into a million.*

---

*For a discussion of this market action, see Jim Maratta, "Strictly Educational", *The Market Chronicle,* New York, June 1, 1978.

In the '60s, there was less to lose in the market by playing the growth stocks than other alternate investments. A growth stock purchased at a P/E of 25 could perhaps go no lower than a P/E of 15. One of the cyclical stocks purchased at a P/E of 10 could conceivably fall to a P/E of 5. In the long run, the investors in the growth issues were the big losers, but in the short run, they had their day. A wise investor today will base his fundamentals on the long run, and recognize the changing characteristics and moods of the market through this view. In the short run, it is better to be smart than right, and the game the market is playing may be the only one in town. Of course, most of these growth stocks of the '60s were at the extremes of the market, with P/Es of 50+ (and it has already been noted that a superior return is available through the central market). However, being conservative often is not adequate to maintain a reasonable return from the market, and it is much better to realize that the market is not for investing, than to insist on your market approach at all cost. Facts don't move the market. They never have and probably never will. **It is only what investors think are the facts that has any motivating power, through the actions of the investors.**

There is a constant flow throughout the market. An industry is strong one day, and next it appears to be disintegrating. One method of viewing this improvement and decline is shown in Figure 2-2. Here the current P/E (market position) has been plotted against the long term P/E (market inertia) for a group of stocks. We would normally expect some small variability, such as the lower line. There is higher variability with the higher P/E stocks, as would be expected. An improving industry might be shown by the upper line, where the low P/E stocks have been upgraded by the current market action. A declining industry might be shown by the reverse, where the enclosed area below the dotted line is larger than that above.

In 1975, the Congress took some steps to improve the structure of the securities markets with the Securities Acts

Figure 2 - 2
MARKET INERTIA

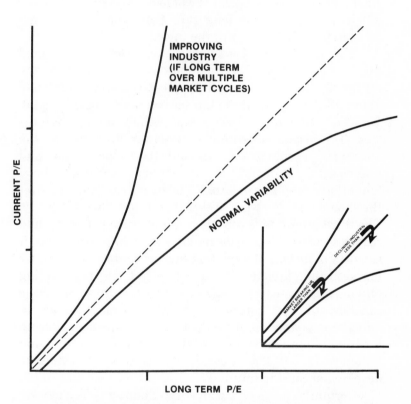

Amendments. The SEC, charged with the functioning of the new laws, proposed an evolutionary process, whereby a slow and steady process of change would be the most healthy for the market and its customers. By 1978, little had happened in substance. The SEC now appears to be more motivated toward direct requirements for conforming with the intent of the law (rulemaking), and through '78 there will be some minor changes in affiliations. None of these changes will affect the individual investor to any large degree. Perhaps a limit order will be executed somewhat more effectively, but any price difference will be too small to be really noticable. Proposed by Congress is a National Market System (NMS), a single front presented to the investor, presumably so that wherever an order is entered, it would be executed at the most efficient point. In the long run, that single front could develop to the detriment of the investor.

The national market system, as now envisioned, could take three forms. The glamourous alternative is the computer based system, where most trades are executed automatically, without the taint of human hands. Forget it. We won't see it anytime soon, and perhaps not through the '80s. The second alternate is a power grab by the big "primary" exchanges to expand their operations, and absorb the "fringes", as the other exchanges have laughingly been referred to. With the country looking over the shoulder of Congress so closely, this one also is unlikely. The third alternate is the one being pursued currently, and requires the least loss of current power to the participants. It consists of linking the existing market centers, so that any market is available to an order. In effect, it is substituting official communication channels for the normal arbitrage function of the market. It may shorten the lag in adjustments, and minimize the inequities that occur during a period of maladjustment. In the short run, the changing structure is not too important. It is wise to watch its development in the future.

Certainly, parts of the Over-the-Counter (OTC) market could be seriously debilitated by the new proposed structure. It is estimated that 800 of the 2200 NASDAC stocks would qualify for the National Market System (NMS), and the management and directors of these companies would have no say as to whether these companies would trade on the NMS or OTC. If qualified, they would trade on the NMS. Some of the stocks might lose their market makers, because of other technical requirements on the NMS. Thus the 800 could lose their market makers, and the 1400 could become second class citizens in the eyes of the public. Other OTC stocks that are not listed on NASDAC currently might also face a degradation of quality and volume in trading by being excluded from the NMS.*

The '75 act did effect a major change, with the elimination of fixed commissions. The transfer of power was from the brokers to the institutions. It accelerated the centralization of the market, much to the market's detriment. With the transfer of power goes the control of greater funds flow (or perhaps the funds flow is the power). The decreasing commission revenues of the brokers has resulted in fewer analysts looking at the market, so that the depth of review is diminished. This may bode well for the individual investor who might have contact with smaller companies, and will find reduced market competition. But he will also find a reduced market, more centralized in fewer issues, and the overall health of the market must suffer from this direction of change.

As the market moves from the growth issues where experience has been so disasterous, securities might hereafter bear some relationship to their economic worth as businesses. In the long run that will happen. In the short run, it is more likely that the market will simply settle at a new level, and it will be only incidental that it might be near a fundamental value. In the bear markets of '73-'74 and '77-78, billions were lost. But it was really only business as usual. The reason we noticed so closely is that now the money is clustered in the major funds, which are more publicly accountable. The losses, therefore, are much more visible. The levels of violence in the market are not over, but they have discontinued their rise. It may be some time before we see the direction change toward reduced gyrations, but by the late '80s, we may again have a market for investing. In the meantime, it is possible to fulfill investment objectives

*For example, see comments by Ralph P. Coleman, Jr. in "Across-the-Counter", *OTC Review,* May 1978.

through this speculative medium. It requires an in-depth knowledge of the market and its vagaries, careful and conservative selection of individual issues, and effective timing to use the market vacillations to support potential for capital gain, or at least minimize potential capital loss in the individual issues.

Chapter 3

The Fudiciary Responsibility

*Why the performance of money managers
often falls short of market averages.*

Assume for the moment that you are a money manager, and you have just been given your own fund. You have an alert and competent research staff, and your own shiny computer that speaks Wall Street. Now that you are so well prepared, you are given about $500 million as your very own plaything.

You've studied hard to reach your position, and you know, in general, the economics of the current market, market action and reaction in detail, and the structural operation of the market. Your capable staff now tells you, and you agree, that the market is on the way down. The market has been booming to all time highs, and the general mood of the street is complete optimism. But the market has overreacted, and dark economic clouds are appearing on the medium term horizon. The market is as yet too enticed by their revelry to have seen them, but it won't be long now. There are few really safe havens in the market, and the defensive stocks seem to offer only a relative safety, and the prospects of large chunks of your capital being gobbled up by the market are large. Interest rates have risen with the current market boom, but with their typical lag. Long term rates lag even more, and it appears that bonds are also headed for a downward adjustment, to allow an increased yield more in line with alternative media.

It is not a time for investing. Everything will be all right in six months to a year, but to enter the market now is suicide. In a short time, the primary market will have made a major downward adjustment, and the stocks will be yielding a more reasonable return, in terms of today's market. That is, after all, your real objective: to invest the money entrusted to you to provide a reasonable return. That return is also your protection against downside risk (loss of capital), knowing that a reasonable return will allow you to stick with a particular issue, even though market action might force the price below what you consider a reasonable value. Within a year, the long term bond market will sort itself out, and reasonable returns will also be available there. Now is simply not the time to invest in equity securities. It will be impossible to maintain and preserve capital in the short term future.

Well, if the market is really going down, you can short on selected stocks, and provide profit in addition to capital preservation for your customers. Let's see, now, what were the objectives of your fund? Of course, you were going to provide a reasonable return, while preserving capital, by investing in equity securities. General objectives, but specific enough for $500 million. The objectives indicate that the average customer is an individual, probably in the top 30% of economic class, a professional or businessman or his widow, who merely wants to invest the money for a reasonable return. The money is supposed to still be there in twenty years, still earning a return, with perhaps some growth in basic value. The individual investor is not terribly concerned with current return, or he would be in an income fund. He merely wants to receive a return, and participate in the growth of America. Most of all he is searching for security and financial stability.

Now, send out your annual report and prospectus for the fund stating that you are 50% in cash, and 50% in (leveraged) shorts. Your cash is primarily short term securities that provide a small return because the risk is diminished by the short time horizon. That's exactly why you selected them, but such a small return! Within hours after your report hit the street, your scalp would be hanging from a flag pole on the Street. Brokers would malign you for repudiating the market. Your fund salesmen would insist on some action. Your congressman would talk about a quarter of a billion short, and propose some legislation to correct this "abuse" of the market. The management of the firms you shorted (and who are now receiving some undesirable publicity) would reject your valuation, and perhaps "find" some profits to temporarily maintain their market price. The financial press would talk about the rising (excessive) power of the institutions in the market, and their ability to provide "selffulfilling functions", so that excessive shorting would in itself force the market down.

Of course, the latter is typical of the double think the market typically dispenses. If funds were not prevented from going contrary to the market, the expertise and acumen of the money managers would eventually approach a small range of values based on fundamental valuation. The excessive fluctuations of the market would eventually dampen. The excessive pricing that you were facing above would have never happened, in that extreme. The horizon of investing would be extended toward the long term, because of the stabilizing prices, and some reasonable degree of capital maintenance could be assumed by the average investor.

The telling blow to your investment plan would come from your customers. There would be cries of irresponsibility, followed by court suits to force you to "do something", to invest the money rather than merely hold it in cash. The news would spread about your irresponsible actions. Few people would know what you did, let alone understand it, but they would all possess that piece of information that you acted irresponsibly. In a rush would come the redemptions, and seemingly overnight the fund would be at 60% of its original value. It can't be expected that people would hire a money manager, and then be content that he would do nothing. If the investors wanted their money in cash, they could have held it themselves. They hired you to perform a function, and you failed to perform. You were supposed to believe in America every day of every year. It was your job to find the opportunities, whatever the circumstances. After all, ABC Corp. was up a point yesterday (½ of 1%, which it quickly lost today).

If you've ever been in that situation, of being required to "do something", you can have empathy for someone like the U.S. President. He is, of all people, subjected to the extreme pressure to act. Often, any action is the worst course, It may be, and often is, that the free marketplace has already begun action that will cure a problem, and at the same time will correct the structures so that the problem will not repeat. The political alternative is to perform some stopgap measure that will temporarily alter or stop the problem, but that will also cause maladjustments in the institutions, so that the problem will always reappear. The limiting factor is that the natural adjustment of the marketplace takes time, and changes in the long term structure require long term adjustments. Often, those caught in the maladjustments will not wait for a natural correction process. While most would believe in the free marketplace, when a pinch is on those affected decide that the market process needs some assistance. The result of action might be a reduction in the efficiency of the natural selection process. Economic participants in a bind probably walked into it with eyes wide open, knowing there was some associated risk. Should they scream loud enough as a group, they might be saved from their mistakes. It's a nice world to have the potential of high reward that is associated with high risk, but not have to pay the price. It's a weakened economic system that cannot be allowed to act. But the politics of the situation sometimes don't allow that decision - the decision to do nothing.

Your decision not to invest was hardly prudent. Under the "prudent man" rule, a money manager should be guided in his actions and investment selections by what would be appropriate for the logical manager pursuing the best interests of his customers. It is a standard applied by the courts, and yet it is completely misleading, worse than useless. What is prudent is what is fashionable at the time. There was a time when prudent meant conservative, and most investments were in high class bonds, and the concern was who would be the first in line in eventual liquidation. Common stockholders were too far down the list to be considered in a prudent position. The concern was with asset management in business, and market position was more important than a leveraged balance sheet.

Little by little we gained some confidence, companies grew more stable (and larger), and it was discovered that common stock did not self-destruct in a variable economy. It became prudent over time to hold common stock, and not holding it might be considered imprudent investing. Corporate bonds were yielding less than 4% in the decade and a half after the war, while industry was growing at an 8% clip. The size of the return became the security, and if that sounds illogical, it was at least fun. The prudent man would only be invested in the best growth companies, often at a multiple of earnings at 50 or above. It would have been less prudent to be in a more stable company with a conservative P/E around 10.

Today the money manager of an $800 million fund sits with paper losses of $300 million, and the prudence of the situation may have caught up with his excesses. At least he followed the prudent rule of being fully invested, and believing in America 365 days of the year. At most, he succumbed to the prudence of the day. The market may have forgotten about financial responsibility, but excesses are not excesses if you commit your sins in a crowd. Slowly, we may return to a considered financial policy of investing. It is more likely that a new stance will be adopted out of fear, fear of loss, fear of reprisal, fear of not performing, than that it will be brought about by a proper return to financial principles of conservatism.

Our return may be slowed by the distance between the public and the market. It is becoming greater daily, and insulates the concerned from the realities of their status. If they don't know that their pension fund lost $300 million, it will never affect them. Payments into the fund will simply be increased sometime in the future. Sometime. The events of the market are now at least once removed from the average public interest. New laws tend to increase the concentration of investing with the institutional investor. A tax exempt retirement fund is not tax exempt unless the individual investor is isolated from his funds. We couldn't allow him to manage the fund himself. He might fritter it away on useles investments. But how do we explain the almost 40% loss of capital that the professional produced for him? It would be difficult to explain to the individual why he is penalized for being an individual.

The individual might just decide that liquidity was safety, and put the entire fund into a savings account. Under the law, he would make about 2% per year less return than a money manager could by trading in commercial paper. It's not a price for safety at all. The risk of illiquidity is probably higher in the savings account than in the commercial paper market. It's the premium the individual investor must pay for the performance of the professional, and that performance has been terrible. In the long run, he has taken the investor into a risky market stance, and lost a considerable amount of the original capital. In the short run, he has demanded, and received his "toll" position in return for his miserable performance. (A toll position exists when a person must be paid for non-service, based solely on his position. He extracts a toll from all who might be required to pass his way.)

An example of the toll position of the money managers is the method of renumeration. It is illegal for their fee to be based on the return of their investments. Typically they base their fee on a percentage (e.g. 1/2 of 1%) of the assets they manage. It might be that a fee based on the return of the fund would encourage excess speculation by the money managers, but in the long term more rational investment policies would always provide the superior return. Legally, the investor is prohibited from seeking a capable fund manager by providing incentive for effective performance. It should not be too surprising that money managers have done less well than the market managers.

But in defense of the professional manager, the safety through liquidity route is not now open to him. He has allowed himself to be drawn into a no-win situation, by foregoing financial principles in times past. In the scenario above, the manager's scalp flew from that flagpole not

Figure 3 - 1
MUTUAL FUND LIQUIDITY

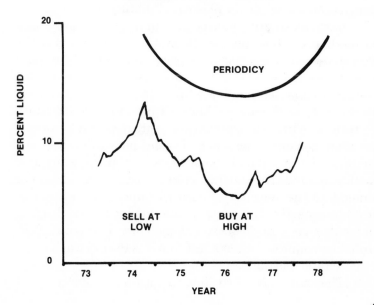

because he wanted to be liquid, but that he wanted to be liquid at the wrong time. When the market is at a high, there is great euphoria, and no one stops to consider that it is the most opportune time to sell, It is, in fact, the only time to sell. The poor money manager is not allowed that tactic, and is actually forced in precisely the opposite position from what would be the most profitable. This is shown in Figure 3-1, where the past liquidity of mutual funds is charted over time. The most liquid position was at the market low in '74, indicating that the fund managers were selling most heavily at a market trough. The lowest liquidity was during the market height in '76. It is uncanny that they could be so precisely counter to a profitable trading tactic, buying high at the peak, and selling low in the trough.

It is a carefully considered strategy to appeal to new funds coming into the market. When the market is booming, a fund must be fully invested in the peaking stocks. And when the market is full of gloom, the fund must be at maximum liquidity. This approach is necessary to appeal to the potential customers of the fund. A fund must be able to send its salesmen into the field with the story that the fund is fully participating in a successful market, and providing adequate protection against the market vacillations in the bear market. After a rise of a group of stocks, if the fund wasn't invested, it must acquire these issues for its portfolio. The money manager will buy the high priced issues for his portfolio, even though he knows that they are currently overpriced. When a prospectus goes out, at least it looks as if the management is superior. The primary goal is to sell funds, and to do that it must appeal to an investor at a particular time. The purpose is to do better than the other funds, and the objective of outperforming the market can never be considered as primary. A manager must sell off his bad paper so that it doesn't appear on the books. That probably means selling at a loss, but it is the price of having a marketable portfolio.

The manager also has a personal objective of

outperforming the other funds. In investing, the primary motivation is: not to look stupid. Superior performance of the fund in relation to the market is secondary, and it is likely that the manager never gives direct thought to capital maintenance. It's not his money, and the pressure of public money management is more than an average investor could comprehend. The controlling motivation of the money manager is to reduce the visibility of his stupidity. No one can consistently outperform the market, and the longer the time period considered, usually the worse the record.

Money managers manage cash, not stocks. Dealing with cash, they are dealing with paper. The value behind the issues is often lost, and transactions are movements of pieces of paper. There is no such thing as a price that is too high or too low when it comes to pieces of paper, and whatever is in fashion must be in the portfolio. Whatever the market wants at a particular time, it will fight for at any price, regardless of fundamental value. The marketing effort is supreme, and the objectives of a capital market are often lost as a motivating force in fund management.

The analysts need to change their conceptual approach to the market, but it cannot happen so easily. The customers, the ones with the money, simply will not allow it. It is not only individuals who are investing in mutual funds that force a cyclical approach counter to profitability. The corporate financial manager who would oversee his pension fund often acts likewise, in forcing the fund to appeal to the emotionalism of the market. He too must answer to his board of directors who have little appreciation of the technical side to investing. They want to see the glamours in the portfolio, at any price, and so the fund management can either follow their wishes or lose the management position. This portion of the market, the pension funds, grows larger daily, with an infusion at $10 billion annually. It sometimes overwhelms its parents, the corporation. It is estimated that the net pension liability of the steels is almost $6 billion, out of a total equity of only about $18 billion. This unfunded liability poses a threat of primary importance in the future, over the considerations of economic operations. It is estimated that even now, certain plants cannot be closed, even though operating inefficiently, because of the potential pension funding that would be immediately incurred.

The overinstitutionalized state of money management grossly ignores the basic concept of intrinsic value in securities valuation. The basic objective is not one of investing, but of developing a marketing stance. Somehow, the basic purpose of profitability has been lost in dealing with the nonprofessional. This portion of the market steadily grows larger. The combination of mutual funds, investment companies, bank trust funds, private pension funds, foundations, college endowments, state and local retirement funds, and insurance funds are creeping towards half of the total stockholdings in the U.S. There is also excessive turnover, so that about 75% of the total trading volume comes from this ill-motivated group. They have typically done less well than the averages in the '60's and '70's, and little correction appears to be in store for the '80's. At best, the Dow from '62 to '75 broke even, if deflated by the wholesale price index. The funds, over time, have not even preserved their capital.

The centralization of funds in the market, over the short term, will lead to increased vacillation, if they continue to be motivated by the emotionalism of the market. If the funds could really carry a complete cash portfolio, the gyrations of the market might develop to the point where they could be completely self-destructive. Fortunately, a 40% cash position is excessive, with a 20% cash position representing high liquidity, so the managements are limited in the game they can play. Over the long run, the basic objectives of investing will return, as most systems return to basics, and responsible investment policies will bring about a gradual slowing of the excessive vacillations that we are currently experiencing.

Part II
Timing

Timing is all important in the market. The investor can take excessive risks and select the wrong stocks and still invest successfully if the timing is appropriate. This timing involves finding the right time to sell as well as the right time to buy.

The key to timing is the development level of the market, and it is best measured by the depth of the market. At the beginning, in the trough of a market cycle, many investors have left the market, and withdrawn their funds. The market prices are at a relative low, and volume has been declining. As investors begin to realize the oversold condition of the market and the excellent buys available, they are also looking ahead to increased economic activity in the near future. There is a surge of volume and activity that starts prices rising. This point is the strongest part of a market, as rising prices are expected in a growing economy and the market is reacting to the oversold position of individual stocks.

Eventually, a slowdown occurs and a reversal, or correction takes place. At this point, stocks typically are around their reasonable long term value. However, the rising market and reasonable values brings in additional investors. Volume is particularly strong, the strongest that occurs throughout the market cycle. The market moves up again, but the new investors begin to crowd the popular securities. Sophisticated investors first, then others following begin to search for better prices on issues. The investors slowly move from the large corporations of the Fortune 100 to successively smaller companies in search of better buys. Thus, the market does not rise in a single move; it rises in a slow ripple effect, like dominos falling.

Toward the peak of the cycle, volume is beginning to decline. Prices have become too high for fundamental investing, and yet they continue to rise. The activity is intense, though beginning to thin, and slowly the rise slackens, and then stops. It is a short time before investors realize that the stocks they hold are overpriced, and a general price decline ensues, on moderate volume. The market pauses, typically near its fundamental value, which is higher than in the rising market because of the improved level of the economy and corporate earnings. Still, the beginning of a market decline precipitates additional sales, and volume becomes high, second only to the peak at the midpoint of the rising market. The market continues down, below a reasonable level of value, until halted by the excesses of the overreaction, and a new trough is formed.

The investor must not make the mistake of equating the market cycle just described with the business cycle. They are entirely different with different characteristics and different timing. The market cycle typically leads the business cycle, though the length of lead has been changing with changing conditions. And within that cycle, general moods and economic conditions of the country change the general level of the market prices. The investor competent to select fundamental values must be aware of the times in which he is investing and their characteristics.

That's the real world. It doesn't always fit the theory, and is constantly changing its character. In that real world it is possible for the investor to buy stocks at reasonable value, so that a reasonable return is received. The investor must simply use his normally developed economic acumen and refuse the purchase of stocks at an inflated value. Stocks purchased at a fundamental value are always timed correctly, but it is possible to purchase stocks at less than that fundamental value. This, then, is the importance in timing: to use the vacillations of the market to receive exceptional values. Timing such as that is the primary requirement for a highly successful investment program.

Chapter 4

Market Segment

The real world functioning of the market.

In financial theory, and in actual practice, the (potential) return on an investment is related to the risk assumed in making that investment. There is no directly correlated function that defines this relationship, because each investor sees the risks of a particular investment differently. There is, however, a quite definable area of relationship in which it is obvious that this risk/return relationship is the dominant consideration in market valuation.

The market always goes to extremes, and this relationship is no exception. At one end of the market is the investor who is trying to escape the risk of the market. This segment of the market is characterized by risk aversion, and the investor is willing to pay a large premium to own a security from this segment. Thus, this market segment provides a minimal return from fundamental value, though the action of the market may provide large gains and losses in capital. The investor seldom gets what he thought he was paying for.

At the other extreme of the market is the investor who can afford to lose his capital, and is willing to gamble it for the possibility of a high gain. This investor is the risk taker who is searching for high returns from the market, and is willing to assume larger risks to obtain that return. Some of these investors receive their large returns, but the risk is high. The average returns from this market segment is often lower than that from the risk aversion or the central market segment.

The central market consists of an essentially mathematical relationship between the risk of a firm and the return allowed by the market. This segment of the market tells the most about the status of the market at a particular time. It defines the general mood of investors, and the requirements they are placing on firms in the market. It is the least desirable investment for an investor using the variances of the market to provide capital gains, because it is less subject to vacillations that occur in individual stock valuations. An investor looking for a "buy" or an "opportunity" will be less likely to find it in this segment, than at the extremes of the market.

These three market segments are shown in Figure 4-1. They are titled primary (risk aversion), secondary (central market), and tertiary (risk assumption) because of the order of their action in the market, as we shall see. In this case, the market segments are displayed using a ranking of the P/E ratios. The primary segment is represented by the higher P/E ratios, where investors are willing to pay a higher price for the more stable earnings flow. In the central market the companies are ranked in accordance with the general perception of risk involved in their operations. This is an essentially mathematical function, and in practice is quite consistent. The slope of this market will often indicate at what stage of development the market lies at a particular time. Of equal importance is the extension of the secondary

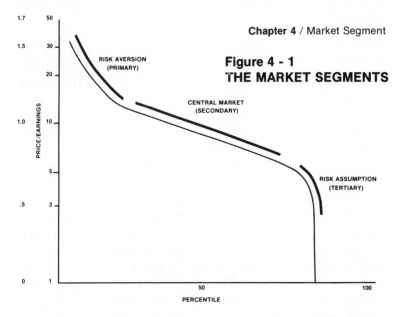

Figure 4 - 1
THE MARKET SEGMENTS

RISK AVERSION
(PRIMARY)

CENTRAL MARKET
(SECONDARY)

RISK ASSUMPTION
(TERTIARY)

PRICE/EARNINGS

PERCENTILE

segment into the extremes.

The tertiary market is a highly volatile one, with as much as up to half of it consisting of companies reporting losses. This is the favorite game of the speculator, searching out "turn-around" situations, in which a company reporting a loss in previous periods is able to generate a profit, and thereby make a large improvement in its market position. These companies are often start-up companies that finally reach a breakeven point. Other companies in this market segment are older firms that have highly volatile earnings flows, or perhaps have an insecure market position.

Special situations exist at any one time in all segments. The data shown is not pure. A typical secondary stock might be located in the primary segment because of a temporary lapse in profit. This might occur because of a one-time writeoff that is essentially a move to strengthen the company, such as closing an unprofitable line of business. It might retain its price, but the decline in earnings would increase the P/E, and push it into the primary segment. Alternately, a particularly large writeoff might result in the company even temporarily reporting a loss, and it could be thrown into the tertiary segment, even though market perception typically places the firm in the secondary segment. There are numerous other situations that occur within the market that might place a particular stock temporarily in a segment to which it did not permanently belong. It is enough that an investor realize that the data is impure, and must always be carefully evaluated.

Using the concept of these three market segments, it is possible to view market movements. In figure 4-2 is shown the general action in a rising (bull) market. At the bottom (A.), the market is relatively flat, because the entire market is suppressed, and fundamental values are supporting the market in general. The central segment is extended far into the primary segment of the market, because of the fundamental support. The negative P/E portion of the tertiary segment (companies with negative earnings) may be relatively large.

With the business cycle declining, confidence is low, and the market begins its upturn primarily as a reaction to the overreaction of the previously declining market (as explained in Chapter 1). In this climate, the marginal investors who reenter the market, or begin upward bidding, want most to protect their investment. They naturally turn to the more stable companies in the primary market (B.). It then begins a slow movement upward, even while the other segments, particularly the tertiary may still be declining.

As investors see the market begin an upward move, and begin to realize the fundamental values built into the depressed market, additonal marginal investors enter the market as well. However, the primary market is not the fundamental buy it was at the bottom, and as confidence returns, investors search the market for a better investment. By now the market is in a definite rising stage, and the secondary market begins its slow rise (C.), in a catch-up to the primary segment. During this stage, the business cycle catches up with the market and begins an upturn instilling further confidence in the market, and causing a deeper

Figure 4 - 2
THE MARKET RISE

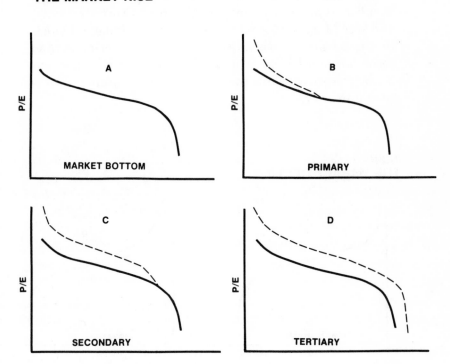

search for more fundamental values.

As the market continues its advance, investor overconfidence pervades the market, and investors begin moving into more risky stocks in the tertiary segment (D.). At this point, business is good, and many of the volatile issues are reporting good earnings. As the investors search the depths of the market there are high fundamental values to be found, if a long range view beyond the standard business cycle of 4+ years is not required. The busines cycle is now in full swing, and the negative sector of the market is growing smaller.

55

At the peak of the cycle, the market slope is much steeper than it was at the bottom. The market may be overconfident, but it retains its essential underlying characteristic of risk aversion. It places a premium on the stability of the primary, and secondary stocks, while relying on fundamental vaues in the tertiary market. At this point, the primary and secondary stocks may contain high market risk, perhaps being overpriced, while the tertiary stocks contain business risk, primarily.

Figure 4 - 3
THE MARKET DECLINE

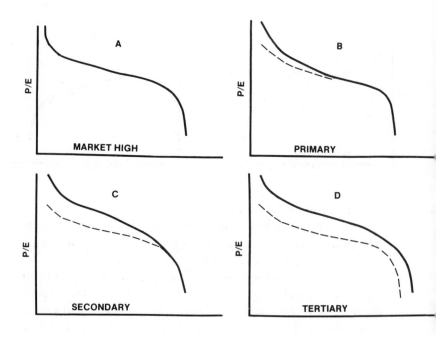

Much the same sequence of events occurs in a declining (bear) market, as shown in figure 4-3. The primary market moves first. It usually has the more knowledgable investors, and the information about the companies involved is much more available. The idea might have been gained that the primary segment consists of large companies. Certainly, a large portion of it may be large firms that have a strong market position, and therefore exhibit the stability of earnings required. Size, however, is not a sole criteria. As an example, consider the conglomerates that have been so marked down in price by the market. They have the size to dominate their markets, but investors have realized that these companies take from the investor an important investment decision: that of selecting a portfolio to diversify risk. Each investor feels differently about the risk he wishes to take and what the future prospects will be for the different industries. Buying a conglomerate issue is like trying to find a mutual fund that reflects your investment objectives. There probably isn't one that matches them. Add to that the fact that the earnings consistency of the multi-industry companies has been inconsistent, and their devaluation in the market is understandable.

In a market decline, the movement is much faster than in a rising market. Given the lag of the business cycle, many of the tertiary companies are reporting their best profits even as investors are searching the market for better protection. The decline is started primarily by a reaction to the overpricing of the market at the high. As investor confidence is lost, the market begins to revalue the earnings flows. The excessive premium paid for stability begins to lose its luster, as the business cycle slows in its later stages, and the hoped-for increases in earnings are not forthcoming. The tertiary segment is more based on fundamental value, these companies are the slowest to profit by the business cycle rise, and so market pressure downward is less in this segment.

Eventually, the busines cycle will catch up with these

companies, and the market will work its way through the three segments. The market will be back at its bottom, where it was joined in Figure 4-2. It is relatively flat at this point, and the negative sector is relatively large. It is at this low that there are often variances in the market function that can be used to the advantage of the knowledgable investor. At this point money is being withdrawn, and investors are

Figure 4 - 4
INTEREST RATES AND MARKET CYCLES

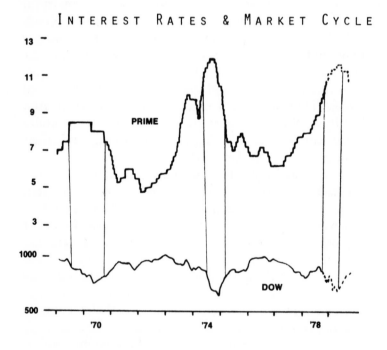

retreating from the market. The market is somewhat unresponsive to news and events and situations. At the high of the market, an earnings improvement might be completely absorbed by the market in 45 days. In a market low, price improvement might come as late as 90 days. Of course, there is an initial price move on such information, but research has indicated that a completely "efficient" market does not exist. **The market is usually less efficient at the lows.**

It's worthwhile to look more closely at the trough, and the tertiary of the bear and the primary of the bull that help to form it. The stock market is a financial market and as such is most strongly influenced by monetary policy. The idiocy of federal fiscal policy in the seventies has forced monetary policy into excesses that have directly increased the vacillations of the stock market. The general form of the interest rate cycle is a broad based "U", and it is growing steadily more intense. The general form of that cycle as represented by the prime rate is shown in figure 4-4. Note that while the base is reasonably wide, the peaks are where policy actions become excessive. They are the result of (ineffectual) attemps to use monetary policy to control inflation without an attendant fiscal policy!

At the low end of the cycle the FED is in much the same situation as the money manager of Chapter 3. Should they start to tighten policy at an early stage as an anticyclical policy, they would be accused of choking off the recovery; Congress would hold hearings, and likely the independence of the FED would be lost. Yet, there is a lag between monetary policy action and its reflection in the business cycle and, of course, the stock market. Just as the money manager must operate contrary to profitable action, so must the FED delay their actions from an approptiate time. When they do act, it must be strongly. It forms the excessive peaks of the interest rate cycle and reinforces the business cycle.

Note that the interest rates being considered are short term rates. They are much more volatile than long term rates. We typically think of time as a risk factor, and envision the interest rate maturities curve (February 28, 1977) in figure 4-5. That was at the bottom of the interest rate cycle. With monetary policy primarily directed at short term funds, this section vacillates strongly with a move of up to 6 points while long term rates move less than 1. The result is an inverted interest rate maturity curve such as the two shown for '74 and '78. (The '78 curve is not a peak.)

Figure 4 - 5
TREASURY SECURITIES

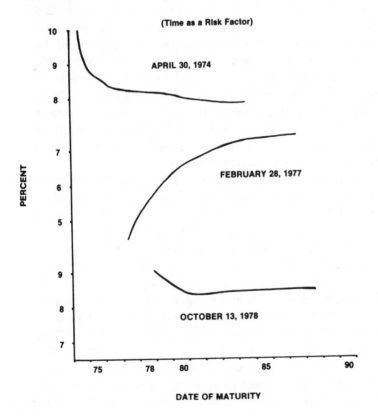

That has a very direct effect on the stock market. Consider that there are two types of funds in the market, money market (short term) funds and capital market (long term) funds. The short term funds will move toward the best return much more quickly than the long term funds. As short term interest rates rise and the maturity curve becomes inverted, these funds flow out of the stock market forming the tertiary of the bear. When interest rates then drop so presipitously, they flow back into the market forming the primary of the lull. This relation is shown in Figure 4-4.

These two movements are the strongest of the market, and also form the point when fundamental value becomes the floor of support for prices. The real threat to the market is that additional capital funds will become short term in search of the excessive short term rates, while long term rates lag the steadily rising trend of inflation. Of course this is exactly what has been happening, and why we face the increasing pulsations shown in Figure 1-3. Some short term money is required to stabilize the market by arbitrage and flows in and out. However, it appears that from an already excessive twenty percent of the 60's the market now has mobilized up to forty percent of its funds for short term movements. **There is the potential for a level of violence that an orderly market cannot withstand.**

Interest rates also have a secondary but more fundamental effect on market prices. This is through the long term rates. Even though they move much less than short term rates, they can have a strong reinforcing effect on the tertiary of the bear and primary of the bull. A price is determined by earnings potential discounted at a required rate of return (e.g., $P = E/i$). Ignore for the moment consideration of quality of the earnings. As long term rates (i) increase the price level of the market will decline. It should be noted that at this time Federal policy is to slow the business cycle. Since the market leads the business cycle (E is potential earnings), E is declining

61

while i is increasing. Added to the outflow of short term funds the market decline is exceptionally strong.

It might be worthwhile to look at an actual example of the movements of the market segments. Theory is of value to the investor, but it will seldom be explicitly carried out in practice. There are far too many variables in the market and the economic scene for a single presentation of market operation to fully explain the market action. It should also be noted that this is how the market has acted in the past, and changing conditions will change the action of the market. It is important to remember the reasons for the market actions. That is why the presentation of the market segments can be an effective tool, for it presents the changing mood of the market.

In spite of that warning, you will find a surprising fit to the action of the market segments in the last full market cycle (1970 to 1974). This is shown in Figure 4-6, along with the action in the current market cycle (1974 to 1978). The heavy lines show the salient market actions. Note particularly the reaction from the 1970 low, the move to the 1973 peak, and the move to the 1974 low. None of these are part of the general market action. What that means to the investor is that they would be very difficult to forecast. This approximate 10 percent on the bottom and top of the market cycle is fraught with excessive risk. There is seldom a consistent market action in this portion of the market cycle, and the movement has often been opposite to the direction taken in this particular cycle. Each cycle is different and motivated by different factors. The general mood of the market, the causal factors, and the specific economic events preclude this area for investing to the rational investor. That does not mean, of course, that a particular stock might not be highly attractive at this time. It is not a time when reliance can be placed on the general market movement.

Note that the successive stages of the market action (from primary to secondary to tertiary) become steeper in slope. Not only are the underlying

Figure 4 - 6
MOVEMENTS IN THE MARKET CYCLE

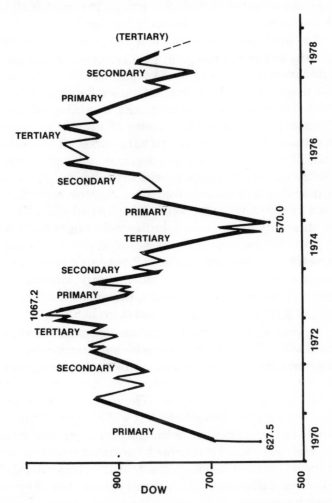

companies more volatile, but the general consensus of the market is gaining strength toward a paticular direction. The underlying actions of the business cycle also accentuate this action, as the business cycle catches the market cycle and reinforces its actions. It always takes a while to get a force as diverse as the market moving. Once it is moving, it reinforces itself, and it takes a strong factor, such as fundamental value, to halt the action. The market always overreacts in its panic to follow the general action.

An intelligent investor will use the three market segments to his advantage in his investment program. He would invest in blue chip stocks at the bottom turning point of the market cycle. As the market paused for an adjustment, he would search for secondary stocks, accepting additional risk in a particular stock because of decreasing general market risk. A second pause in a bull market might indicate a market euphoria that would decrease risk sufficiently to allow the investor to accept the risk of the "dogs". These may continue climbing in price even after the general market (as shown by the Dow or S&P500) has begun to decline. The lag in profitability to the more volatile stocks might carry their sell point far into the primary segment down movement. Where the typical market cycle is 2½+ years rising and 1½+ years declining, an investor intelligently shifting from segment to segment would find a rising market for over 3 years, of a typical 4 1/3 year market cycle.*

Of course, each market cycle must be carefully studied individually. There are cycles in which the tertiary segment move never materialized as a separate market movement. It was blended into the secondary, or high risk factors dampened it to minimal action. The purpose here is not to give a dogmatic statement of what will happen. That's not possible in the market. It is the purpose to present casual relationships that are tied to the basic impetus of the market and the investment function. The causal factors will exhibit themselves differently at different times, but they will always be present.

---

*For an example of an application of the market segments to an industry, and the general market action within that industry, you may wish to refer to Figure 10-3, and the attendant discussion.

Chapter 5

Cycles

Consistent inconsistency.

The market has a basic rhythm that has existed for as long as records have been kept. Some people would insist that the rhythm is a cycle, a continuing oscillation that tends to perpetuate itself. The correlations of actual data to the theory of a cycle or cycles are never too high, but this may be only an indication of their imprecision, not of their lack of existence. Certainly, evidence of periodicy does exist in stock prices.

In fact, this periodicy is stronger in the stock market than in other related activities. The market would seemingly be based on economic activities, such as the general level of the GNP. This would include such things as the effect of price changes, and the general fluctuations of the dollar (in terms of purchasing power) that have generally occurred throughout our economic history. However, the processes of the two (the market and the economy) are not the same. In economic ventures, decisions are subject to the requirement of economic viability, and failure to make a profit results in a natural weeding-out process that strengthens the economic structure and the entities involved. Those that remain over the long term probably are serving a basic need of the general market, and have a basic purpose and committment that is a stabilizing influence.

In the stock market, there is no such stabilizing influence. The purpose of the stock market is to provide capital for business operations, and as such, it should be a long term operation. In such a case, an investor would invest in a firm, and the market would reflect the slow growth or decline of that firm. In a successful firm growing at about 12% per year, the market valuation would reflect that growth, less the dividends paid. This valuation would be subject to minor vacillations wrought by long term changes in the busines climate that would increase the desirability of one industry over the other, or similar business opportunities.

That is not the real world. In operation, the market has come to act like a money market (versus a capital market) and is short term in nature. There is a failure to consider fundamental business values, and decisions are often entirely emotional. The vacillations that occur from such decisions tend to reinforce themselves. Fundamental investors cannot find a place in the market, while speculators often profit from activities completely unrelated to the underlying business operations. Small variations in the business cycle are highly magnified in the market, and it becomes an essentially unstable activity.

Add to that the fact that the market acts in anticipation of the flow of the economy, and the market picks up a regularity that cannot always be seen or often does not occur in business operations. This regularity flows from the overreaction and anticipation by the market. A single event sends the market out of balance, over or underpriced.

In anticipation of events inadequate to support that price level, the market reacts toward the other extreme. Sometimes this wave is reinforced by economic events, but it is not always necessary to cause an overreaction in the opposite direction.

That helps to explain the amplitude to the business cycle, but more perplexing to some is the periodicy, seemingly a relative constant. There is a group that would say that cycles are a phenomenon of nature. There is a Foundation for the Study of Cycles* that studies cycles in all activities. Without attempting to explain the duration, they simply attempt to ascertain what the duration is. They study cycles in the weather, prices, human activities, activities of nature, and just about anything that occurs over time that can be assigned a value. They have been so thorough in the stock market that they have discovered as many as two hundred different cycles in stock prices. Recently, their computers have discovered a more basic thirty seven cycles in stock prices. With that much data, the proposal of consistent cycles is probably worthless, unless the investor would wish to blindly let the computer indicate probable trends. It would not be a wise choice. A strong 41 month cycle turned upside down in the fifties, and a stronger 9+ year cycle has failed on the down side since the fifties. It is not too likely an investor would have made money following the "consistent" cycles without reason.

There are definite evidences of reasonably consistent cycles in many areas of human activity. Ask any large city police officer, and he will verify that crime activity increases around the full moon. Alternately, we may consider it a constant cycle, but in fact scientists tell us that the speed of rotation of the earth is changing, and thus those moon cycles. It is only that the change in activity is of such a long

---

*Edward R. Dewey (President of the Foundation), *Cycles - The Mysterious Forces that Trigger Events,* Hawthorne Books, Inc., New York, 1971 is a good introduction to this organization and its studies.

term nature, that our perception is inadequate to note its changes.

Most (and perhaps all) underlying causes of cycles are changing. We all know an engineer who discovered the stock market and its cycles, practiced his Fourier analysis,** lost his money, and eventually left the market. In practice, mathematical cycle analysis is inadequate to provide profit in the market. The engineer requires a formula and then a correlation to that formula. Human activity is seldom exact enough to fit such an approach, particularly when the activity is primarily motivated by emotional decisions. Each cycle of the market, and the economy, is motivated by varying causes, and the mix of these causes is constantly changing. There is no consistent cycle in the market, because the underlying causes are too varied and complex.

The market does have a cyclical nature. It acts in anticipation of events, and often accentuates the underlying economic activities. At the peak of a business cycle, the market typically leads by about 9 months. At the trough, the market typicaly leads by about 6 months.* Those are average post war figures. In the last twenty years, the lead of the market has become smaller. That may be a good sign, indicating an increasing reliance by the market on fundamental values.

**A mathematical method of cycle analysis. As an example, it would be used by communication engineers to determine the components and harmonics of a radio frequency wave. Applied to stock market cycles, it would separately define the two week, seventeen week, eighteen month, fourplus year, nine year, etc. cycles that combine to form the general market picture. No one that I know of has ever been able to successfully predict the market from this type of research (and I know many capable engineers who have tried). The cycles, if they exist, are too inexact for mathematical manipulation over time.

The basic underlying business cycle is just over four years. It has been as short as three years and as long as almost five years in the post war period. The minimum and maximum lengths are primarily the result of leads and lags in economic operations. Most causes take about a year and a half to filter through the vertical structure of the economy. It takes about a year and a half to two years for lumber price changes to be reflected in the resale market for housing. It takes about a year for a change in interest rates to be fully effected, after a six months lag from the cause to the initiation of the action. It takes about six months for a change in fund flows to be fully reflected throughout the banking system, and another six to nine months for this flow to be reflected back through bank activities, in their effect in the economy. The list goes on and on. There are also longer term lags, but it takes, as a minimum, about a year and a half for the inertia of a direction to be reversed in the economy.

With the size of the economy and its potential inertia, the cycle itself often feeds back to effect economic activity. Certain actions that exceed the two year turnaround time are often not felt until the following cycle, even though their turnaround time is less than the 4+ year lag. Some analysts note this delay in what is termed a nine year cycle. It does

---

* Additional information on leads and lags of stock prices is available in the monthly *Busines Conditions Digest,*Bureau of Economic Analysis, U.S. Department of Commerce. In their "Experimental Data and Analyses" they are able to go beyond the standard approach of statistical correlations, and present data that might have logical consistency although lacking in mathematical precision. A less technical presentation of leading and lagging indicators, including stock prices, is available in the semi-monthly *Investment Bulletin,* American Institute Counselors, Inc., Great Barrington, Mass.

appear, discounting the long term trends in the economy, that successive 4+ year cycles do not reinforce. A severe low has been followed by a relatively shallow low. A soaring peak is followed by a subdued activity level in the next cycle. That an overreaction from the trend is followed by a reaction is not too surprising.

The important thing to remember is that our interest is in the market cycle, not the business cycle. A different type of business cycle will have a different effect on the market cycle. A business cycle caused by monetary factors will have the strongest effect on the market cycle. If the underlying cause of an economic change is inflation, it will be felt much stronger in the market, as we are seeing in the late '70's. The capacity utilization and inventory adjustments of the mid '60's did not have a strong effect on the market. **The market cycle is different from the business cycle.** Remembering this fact is an important fundamental in investing.

The medium term periodicy of the market is shown in Figure 5-1. What is shown is the market measured by the Dow. While this is a somewhat narrow measure, the same cycles would be found in the S&P 500 or other typical measure of market activity. The period covered is about 21 years for the five cycles fully shown. You might note from the lower dotted line why the gloom and doomers of the late '70's have been predicting the Dow at 400 before the end of the decade. I would hardly subscribe to such a projection, without support from more fundamental data. What this descending inverted coil (or triangle) does show is an intensifying of market vacillations. Some of the causes will be covered in detail later, but the two primary causes are the large part played by institutions, and the inability of government to (formulate or) execute a timely economic policy. Persistent inflation and the eventual partial withdrawal of institutions will probably place the market in a general downtrend, for at least the first half of the '80's.

There is another cycle of market activity that is used by

Figure 5 - 1
MEDIUM TERM PERIODICY

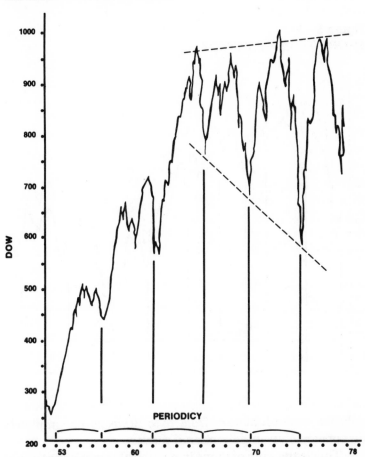

the professional trader. It consists of general trend actions and reactions, and is highly variable for each stock. In terms of the Dow, it is a 17 week cycle that has shown reasonable consistency, over the long term. It is represented in Figure 5-2, over the last several years. This short term periodicy is more volatile than the longer cycles, and is highly subject to significant variations. In individual stocks it is even more

71

Figure 5 - 2
SHORT TERM PERIODICY

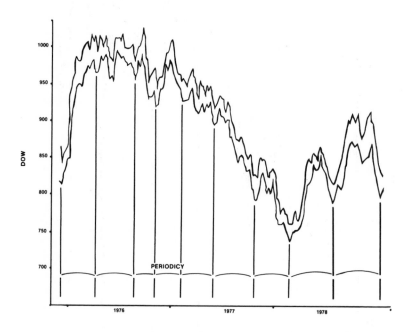

volatile, and might vary from 15 to 19 weeks, or completely disappear in strong directional moves.

This is the kind of move in a particular stock that might be shown most capably by technical analysis. This is assuming that the technical analysis is applied as displaying the general factors of supply and demand, and their development. The short term activity within a particular stock could then be perceived, perhaps, by a capable trader. However, note the stength of the moves of each cycle. It is usually inadequate to more than cover transaction costs for the average trader. While the floor trader can turn a reasonable profit on his high volume on these market moves, the average trader is accepting too high a risk for the small return available to him if he is right. This area of trading is the economic function of the professional trader, who provides an orderly and stable market. It is best left to his expertise.

In the last few decades, the market cycle has been 4½ years, 4 years, 4 1/3 years, 5 years, etc. But it is only consistent in its appearance. Over the long run, the duration, as well as its amplitude, can be expected to change. We would hope that the amplitude would decrease, noting the cycle to be a detrimental factor in long term capital markets. With a seemingly large inflationary trend built in to economic activity, required return in the market will rise. This will depress prices toward more fundamental values. As more is learned about valuation techniques, this increased knowledge will perhaps also have a dampening effect on the market cycle.

It has been resonably easy since the late '60s to see that the character of the market is changing. The go-go days of growth at any price have yielded to some sensibility in price levels. The long term trend of the market peaked in '66, and the trend has been downward since then. With the early stages of a long term decline comes the high vacillations that result from investor uncertainty.

One way to view this changing character is to look at the length and amplitude of the market cycle over time. For example, the length during the post-war period is shown in Figure 5-3. The basis for the chart is the S&P, 500, and assumes a low for the current cycle of 72 in early '79. We have come to think of the market cycle or 4+ years as consisting of a two and a half year bull and a year and a half bear. You can see that, while the total is reasonably constant, the bull move is decreasing and the bear move is increasing, so that we now have both bull and bear moves approximating two years.

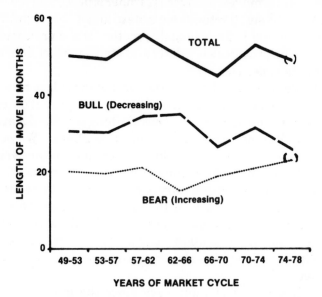

Figure 5 - 3
LENGTH OF MARKET CYCLES

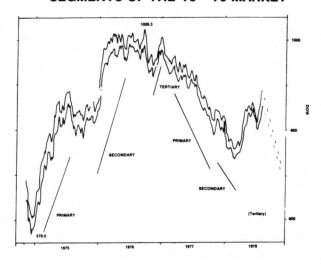

Figure 5 - 4
SEGMENTS OF THE '75 - '78 MARKET

The amplitude chart in Figure 5-5 shows a similarly changing character. The total move of the complete market cycle has been about neutral since the long term trend of the market turned generally downward in '66. The move of the bull market has been generally decreasing, while the bear market has become a stronger portion of the overall market cycle.

Figure 5 - 5
AMPLITUDE OF MARKET CYCLES

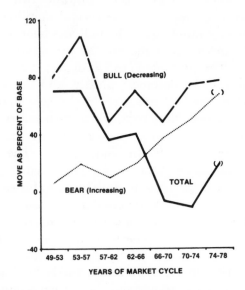

A reminder of the mathematical reality of what happens as the bear approaches the bull. For example:

Bull 100 X 150% = 150
Bear 150 X 50% = 75
Net Change -25%

A 50% increase and a 50% decrease in the two major moves of a market cycle results in a decreasing market total. That has been somewhat the case over the last three market cycles.

The consistancy of the charts depend on how the market is interpreted, of course. I consider the actual high of the Dow in September '76 at 1026.3 as only the peak of the secondary rise, with the January '77 break just above 1000 as the true peak of the market cycle (tertiary peak). This current cycle chart is shown in Figure 5-4 with primary, secondary, and tertiary market segments indentified for both the bull and bear markets.

Some addional detail, the bull and bear primary moves, have been added to the second amplitude chart. As you probably know, both the bull and bear market are divided into three major moves, the primary, secondary, and tertiary. The primary is the strongest, the secondary displays the highest volume typically, and the tertiary is the weakest in the bull market. In the bear market, the strength is reversed. Note that, while the primary remains a large portion of the bull market, the primary has become less and less important in the bear market. (The primary, secondary, and tertiary moves would not add up to, but would typically exceed the total. The base for each move is different, and the reversals must be accounted for.)

If the market cycle was a casual factor, rather than a result of economic activity, speculation on the moves in price would amplify the cycle. Knowledgable investors would be out of the market on the down move, and be buying back in on the up move. Vacillations could be thrown completely out of control. However, the market vacillations are representing basic causes that are not so clearly motivated. Increased knowledge of the cycle in economic activities will allow businessmen and financiers to anticipate the flow of funds and fund availability that occurs, and their anticipatory moves will tend to dampen and lengthen the cycle. Additional knowledge on the part of both business and government will tend also in the long run to lengthen the cycles.

We are currently not there yet. The 1980 budget of the federal government is being proposed at at time of peak business activity, and yet it still initially shows a deficit of $30 billion. By the time Congress acts to add their pet programs, it could grow much larger than that. At a time when inflation is moving upward, such an impetus will cause excessive overreaction. Government is proving that they cannot act in less time than private business, and thus policy cannot cope with a medium term business cycle. By the time an action can be formulated, it is completely out of phase with what it was intended to accomplish. If a reasonable solution can be found to that problem, we could see the cycle becoming less important in the future.

Figure 5 - 6
AMPLITUDE

(with primaries)

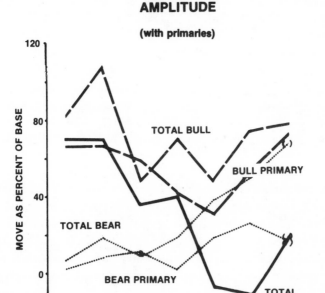

YEARS OF MARKET CYCLE

Part II / Timing

Chapter 6

Moods

Emotions control the market with predictability.

There are some longer waves of action that have a large effect on the market. It is not too surprising that there would be vacillations around the general trend in a imprecise human activity such as the market. We might expect that there would be an overreaction, and a following reaction, which would lead to overreaction in the other direction. These waves of action are less precise than the shorter term cycles. The factors causing them are less direct, and they are in general caused by a prevailing emotional content.

The general prevailing mood in these longer wave actions often defines the trend as well as the vacillations around that trend. In the post-war period, this trend has been strongly upward, both in economic activity and in the market. The growth rate of both has been phenomenal for something over a twenty year period. Now we are entering a period when those growth rates can no longer be sustained. Population growth has diminished, and the GNP growth rate has declined from a general 8% rate of growth to around

3%. Some of the lags from the previous periods, such as the effects of fiscal growth in government and excessive monetary growth have continued to force the monetary sector of the economy into higher action while its requirements have diminished. The result is a building inflationary base which will help to accelerate a monetary downturn in the next decade.

Thus, the general trend in the economy is slowing, and might be perceived as approaching a turning point. In fact, if a market index, such as the Dow, were discounted for inflation, we would find that the market turned down in '66. This is shown in Figure 6-1. Meanwhile, an overreaction in monetary sectors is building that will develop the downward cycle of a long wave. In the long wave, the reactions are slower to develop and decadelong lags are often found. Such lags in the past should have given us time to control the wave more effectively. At a time when it became obvious that the mature structure of the economy was allowing it to slow, appropriate governmental fiscal control should have been provided. Such rational action is not the rule of emotional reaction, and the general decline was not perceived. Rather than merely slowing the economic activity in accordance with demands, it was pushed for continued growth.

The situation which is developing is not unlike the actions of the cities of the Northeast that refused to recognize their problems, such as crime. Inability or refusal to control crime only accelerated the move of productive population segments to the suburbs, and the cities found themselves overtaxing to maintain a structure that was no longer required by a dwindling population. The higher taxes forced additional populations and businesses out of the city, and a vicious cycle was formed that will take years for the cities to resolve.

It seems we have managerial ability only to follow a trend without major change in direction. A reversal is seldom adequately perceived, and when perceived we are

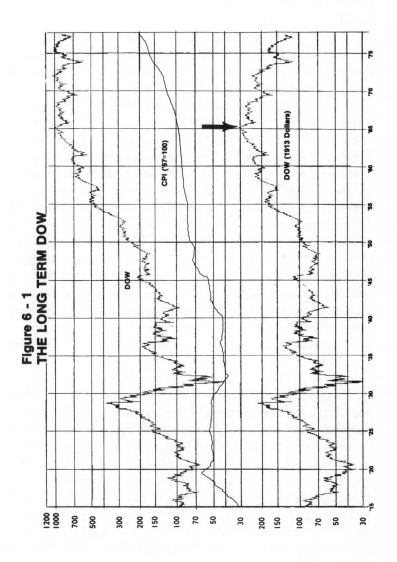

Figure 6 - 1
THE LONG TERM DOW

incapable of adequately reacting to it. Fortunately, businesses react more effectively than political bodies, and this management talent could be very important in the next decade, as we face a trend reversal, or at least a change in trend.

There are technical cyclists who see these trends and moods as a mathematical and consistent action in human events. One such view is shown in Figure 6-2, where the major cycles from 21 weeks to 77 years have been presented. This particular view attempts to explain the recession of 1974, a coming recession in 1979, and a '30's type depression beginning in 1984. The distinction is not clearly made here between the market cycles and the economic cycles, but what is actually shown are the market cycles. Note the market low in December '74, while the decrease in GNP continued through April '75. As Mr. Sullivan points out, the variance in timing is not too important when viewing the long term, but the causal factors can certainly be different, and thus the severity of the two cycles can be highly variant.

The 21 week, the 54 month, and the 9 year cycles were covered in the previous chapter. Here we want to concern ourselves with the longer range cycles, and the general moods that prevail within them. The economic cycle that is best known is the 54 year cycle, sometimes called the Kondratieff cycle,* after the Russian economist who first postulated it. The long wave found was actually 52 years, but the length of the cycle leads to imprecision. The cycle postulates a decreasing rate of inflation, rekindled at short business upswings, but always at decreasing rates. With that prospect, it might be nice to believe in the cycle. It has

---

*Shuman and Rosenau, *The Kondratieff Wave,* Dell Publishing Co., New York, 1972 contains an application of this WWI economic theory to recent events, current operations, and possible future developments. It's in readable form for the non-economist.

Figure 6 - 2
STOCK MARKET CYCLES

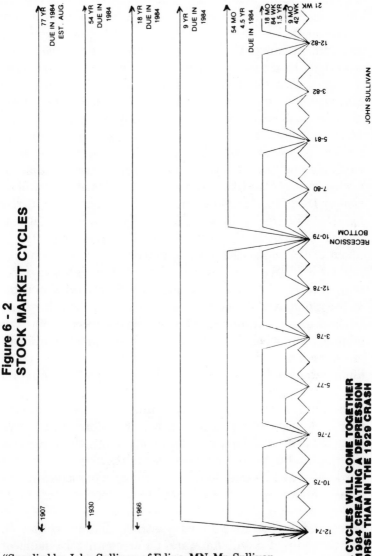

"Supplied by John Sullivan of Edina, MN. Mr. Sullivan is the author, with John L. Preston of *How to Beat the Stock Market Rip-Off,* Hawkes Publishing Inc., Salt Lake City, Utah, 1976. A similar form of the chart is presented in the book."

been explained by present day economists as resulting from an overbuilding (overreaction) of capital equipment, to the point of excess capacity. Business then withholds further investment in capital equipment, and the underlying investment causes the beginning of a decline in ecomomic activity that takes over two decades to reverse.

In the stock market the long cycle has also been discovered. Its duration since the late 18th century has been 44 years, 54 years, 36 years, and 50 years.* That hardly seems adequate support for a cycle theory. It was used to project a Dow of 400 in the 80's. That projection failed to consider one theory of cycles, the nonreinforcing of adjacent cycles. The 1779 to 1835 rise eventually fell to about 2/3 of its rise by 1842. The 1842 to 1889 rise fell to about 1/3 of its rise by 1896. The 1896 to 1929 rise fell to 2/3 of its rise by 1932. It might be expected that the 1932 to 1973 rise would fall to about 1/3 of its rise. That would place a Dow low around the mid 600's. That is not to lend credence to the highly variable long cycle theory, but only to point out the mistakes of some of the gloom and doomers in applying their own theories.

There are some analysts who ascribe the '29 crash as a big mistake. It has been called a political error, an aberration in market economics, or the result of foreign trade mismanagement. Whatever set it off, it was a financial crash, resulting from overextension of markets, and a wandering from fundamental values. It was a money market adjustment, and something that should not have occurred in a capital market. Perhaps, though, there must be a periodic adjustment in values even in the long term capital markets. We sometimes too easily believe in ourselves, given small advances, and the step to a loss of technical

---

*Proposed by Charles D. Kirkpatrick, II and Walter R. Burns, codirectors of the Market Forecasting Division of Lynch, Jones and Ryan and publishers of the BurnsKirkpatrick Market Letter. Their studies are based on the Kondratieff wave, mentioned above.

responsibility seems a small one. The failure to heed the basics of financial control is easy, once the vision of possible consequences if left far behind. Of course, with terrifying speed, these consequences catch up, and the market is snapped back to reality. The adjustment process is necessary, but it is vexing that the price paid for our folly need be so onerous. Of course, it need not be, if we simply heed the lessons of the past, and maintain fundamental value as a basic criteria for investing in capital markets. That's a requirement in the long run. In the short run, a speculator may run with the crowd, but the distinction in functions must always be borne in mind. **The most difficult part of investing is maintaining the comprehensive and long term outlook required in capital markets.**

There has been a recurrent change of moods, with particular phases appearing at approximate half century intervals. Perhaps it is this period that is required for the old guard to retire and exit from the economic sphere, so that a new generation can begin making its own mistakes. Even though the mistake of emotional control of so mundane an activity as a capital market has been repeated time after time, each recurrence is different. It occurs in an environment of different circumstances, and therefore the final result will be considerably different. The technical characteristics change, but the emotional content seems to maintain its character. It would be hoped that some lessons would be learned over time, and each new swing of the moods would be more in tune with the principles of an effectively operating capital market. Maintenance of these principles would dampen the oscillations of the long term moods. No such action is in evidence in the market of the '70's, but there is an increasing awareness among individuals of the potentials of such an approach. Even though the pace is so terribly slow, we are learning about the market action in capital markets. It will take some time before this knowledge can be fully utilized in the markets, but a gradual change will be obvious for those who search for it.

From the euphoria of the '20s, we entered a decade of fear in the '30s. Perhaps a sobering, yet more effective functioning of the capital markets could have come from this experience, were it not for the War. The sobering mood of the '40s turned to some confidence in the '50s, when large technical accomplishments appeared. Unfortunately, the market overreacted as usual, and the confidence turned to a euphoria, and the go-go '60s acted out its foolish play. But a 100 P/E is not a fatal mistake, at least until the stock has to be sold. The investor only gets rich a little slower, as the old saying goes.

Many people have looked back and equated the '20s to the '60s, and forecast depression, devaluation, and general anarchy in the '70s, expecting a recurrence of the action of the '30s. But each change of moods is different, and the structure of institutions has changed in the last half decade. The rife speculation through overextension of financial capabilities did not occur with this mood of euphoria. In the '20s, the overextensions were an individual function, occurring on the individual balance sheet. Currently, the overextensions exist in the balance sheets of the quasifinancial and financial institutions. The liquidity ratio of banks has returned to its level of the '20s. From a loan/deposit ratio of about 75% in the '20s, a '44 level of less than 20% was formed, only to rise steadily to about 80% in the mid '70s. The banking system may be as overextended as it was in the '20s, but the removal from direct participation in economic events imposes a delay in the reaction to events. There is an insulation around the institutions that may give us adequate time to respond to stimuli that otherwise might cause severe economic consequences.

We have been living on credit for some time. The rapid rise in loans mentoned above is akin to the family living beyond its means. Each month they must go to the bank, and withdraw some of their savings to pay the bills for the month. Eventually, the savings will be depleted, even in the most affluent families, and the limits of credit will be reached. The hard realities of economics must then be faced, and the standard of living reduced. Failure to exercise this fiscal control in time for a slow adjustment to the changing conditions will lead to outside pressure that often is applied abruptly. Such an abrupt change is the stuff of which emotional overreaction is made. The market and the economy can be thrown into maladjustment entirely out of proportion to the underlying fundamental values. Delaying such an action by insulation can make the adjustment even more sever, because the problems are deeper and more pervasive before they are recognized. And the final adjustments must then be more basic, to the banks (producer) in the case of credit overextension, instead of individuals (final consumer). Failure of the basic banking system leaves no support whatever. We have been close to failure of system liquidity numerous times. A credit crunch has been a recurring phenomenon occurring in '66, '69 and '74. With inflationary pressures building in late '77 and early '78, it looks like it's "hold on to your hat" time again in '79. The banks have been fortunate to date but they are still seriously weakened. It's not obvious that we can continue turning the wolf from the door.

There are major weaknesses in the banking system. Many of the imprudent Real Estate Investment Trust (REIT) loans of the early '70s have been written off, but many remain without adequate reserves. Loans to lesser developed countries (LDCs) by major banks are beyond the economic ability to repay. Many of the loans to municipalities similarly overextend the bounds of financial reasonableness. Excessive director loans are found throughout the system. The failure of C. Arnbolt Smith's San Diego National Bank and the "discoveries" of the Bert Lance affair are only the tip of the iceberg. There is also increasing fraud, with worthless or more often stolen securities being used as pledge for a loan. When it comes time to repay, the securities are forfeited and the bank takes the loss.

There are some operational weaknesses, also. It is estimated that in ten years the volume of checks will become unmanageable. The electronic funds transfer (EFT) being pushed by the banks is being rejected by the public. If your tight for money, you may prefer to pay a penalty and delay the mortgage payment a few days. EFT removes that option.

The floating exchange rates caused bank failures to increase from an average of about three per year for the thirty years following WWII to 13 in '75 and 16 in '76. The early failure had been the small farmer banks typically, and their failure posed little strain on the Federal Deposit Insurance Corp. (FDIC). By the mid-'70s the failures included banks such as the Franklin National Bank with assets of $5 billion. Other than direct fraud, the biggest reason for failure was foreign currency speculation. The U.S. had removed the gold backing from the dollar in international trade in 1971. The floating exchange rates in '73 could only result in a devaluation of the dollar. Any banker would know that, but they forgot the long time lags are often a decade or more. Two to three years was too short a time to bet against the dollar when other factors served to prop it up in the short term.

In the long run the value of the dollar will be more accurately reflected. With the removal of gold backing we can roll the printing presses and live off the seigniorage, but only as long as other countries accept the dollar. The proposal to establish a European Monetary Fund on January 1, 1979 with a European Currency Unit (ECU) backed by $50 billion in gold and gold backed currencies is most certainly a repudation of our monetary policies. As a monetary phenomenon it can't help but impinge on the market in some way - significantly - in the near future.

Meanwhile, at home we are speedily extending credit to great excesses. In '60 the cash marketable securities on the books of major corporations was 70% of short term (less than 1 year) liabilities. Today it has declined to 30%. This is surely beyond the bounds of financial conservatism, but as long as business is good and the cash flow continues that leverage will work for the companies. Should the economy seriously falter, the leverage can as quickly turn against the company and start a reinforcing slide that neither fiscal nor monetary policy could quickly halt.

A potential for such a business slowdown exists in consumer debt. It has remained at about 20% of after tax income over the last twenty years, but terms have eased, such as 48 month car financing, verses 36 month financing in prior periods. We have simply been borrowing to provide an increasing aggregate demand in the economy. When we reach a limit, excess capacity will exist for that artificial demand. The slowing could be easy, but other factors will play their part. Our mortgage credit has supported excessive price levels in housing. A house that could be built for $35K sells in some areas for twice that amount. Rents are inadequate to support the price, so the owner (speculator) must put money into the project each month. Of course, it's all right because the rising price of the house turns those funds into forced savings. Upward leverage such as that is fine, but it carries the excessive risk of working against the speculator. Tight money or reduced demand from an economic downturn could turn the speculators into bankrupts overnight. All of these factors of excessive credit pose a frightening picture of an economy balanced on too high a beam without a safety net.

Inflation is the main causal factor in the developing downturn of '78. There are those, including some economists, who argue that inflation is preferable to deflation, and therefore some inflation is desirable. That's like calling the Romans magnanimous when they gave the Christians the choice of the lions or the stake. But it does appear that a growing economy can handle short spurts of inflation without excessive harm. The inflation will surely cause maladjustments in price levels, but periods of reduced inflation will allow the economy to adjust to a new level of prices. The price level is reasonably unimportant; it is the changes in price levels that cause maladjustments. If a severe 50+ year ('29 type) low is due, it will not be the downturn of '79. The maladjustments simply don't exist to cause that big a downturn. If inflation continues at a high (historical) level, the imbalances could become great enough to force such havoc. We have a short term to regain fiscal responsibility and soften whatever downturn is due. Unfortunately, we haven't responded to the need for forward planning in the past, and it it doubtful that we will at this point in time.

According to the theory of the long cycle, taxes are pushed to a (relative) maximum at the peak: that is, to the point of nonproductivity. With the tax revolt reaching (although unknown) alarming proportions, and the steady decline of private capital investment as a percent of GNP, we appear to have reached that point in taxation in the '70s. Economically, the high taxes should be a restraint to inflation, and the current level of taxation is just that, it has been argued (but by politicians, not by respected economists). It would be anti-inflationary only if the excess of taxation were used to pay off some of the existing public debt. But the revenue from high tax rates is supplemented by printing press money, in the form of deficits excessive by any criteria. At a time of high economic activity, when receipts are at a relative high,the deficit appears headed for about 20% of the federal government budget. What we are feeling are the long term effects of excessive programs placed into operation long ago. In history, Johnson will probably go down as the inept leader who tried to buy his way into glory with his "social" programs and the great "society". In fact they were economic transfer payments, and had nothing to do with social organization or the functioning of society. What took us so long to build up as an excess will take at least equally as long to undo, without the impetus of an external event, such as a strong economic downturn. The downturn forecast by cycle theory may occur, not because of the mathematical precison of the theory, but because of the necessity to dampen emotional control and return to reality every so often.

If euphoria is required for the final buildup, then some scepticism is required to begin the downturn. It is basically there today, in the form of uneasiness in the stock market demonstrated by increasing vacillations without direction. This can be seen in the form of uneasiness on the part of business managers, demonstrated by reduced investment and investments plans, and in the form of uneasiness on the part of thinking people in general, demonstrated by increasing participation in political and social activities, and yet a reluctance to change direction in any of these activities. Those moods will not cause a major downturn. It is only when these moods become reflected in economic activity that a large downturn could ensue. Most economic participants are too frightened to be so overt, currently. The gloom and doomers have given us a short time of respite, at least, to repair our shortcomings. If we fail to use the time (and it appears we may fail to do so), **the mid-80's will probably yield us the downtown we deserve for our inaction.** Surely, the economic structure will demand strong adjustments in a short time that perhaps can only be accomplished by uncontrolled adaptation.

Of course, we have automatic stabilizers built into our economic operation that would preclude a major downturn, or so the theory goes. There are two major problems with reliance on such stabilizers. First, once put into operation, they become part of the economic structure and are some of the basis on which the economy operates. Unemployment insurance is the most often used example, and it becomes a contributor to personal income. It is basically privately funded, but we have placed continually higher reliance on it, so that it is routine to have a federal extension of benefits. Thus, the economy currently is being propped up by this stabilizer. It is really not capable of adding impetus to a declining economy. An extreme increase in unemployment could be met by payments that would maintain some of the flow of funds into personal income. The source of those funds would either come from a reduced private sector, further suppressing their economic operation by this tax and transfer payment, or it would be supplemented by printing press dollars, increasing inflation, and further suppressing the economic operation of the private sector. It doesn't really appear that the stabilizers would be that stabilizing.

The second problem with the stabilizers is that most would require a trigger by governmental action, to be used effectively at a time of extreme economic adjustment. It has been empirically proven that government has not had the will to act in a timely manner. First it would have to decide that the economic downturn was really severe, then determine what action would best serve (the constituents), and then agree on the form of action. By the time effective action could be taken, it would be inappropriate for the times. In fact, with governmental economic planning, we have seen the business cycle actually increase its vacillations in the last twenty years, rather than subside, as logical "control" should have dictated.

The cycle theory has not proven itself. It postualted a decade of no inflation, along with high prosperity, prior to a downturn. The seventies have refused to cooperate, and inflation has steadily become a stronger depressant on the economy. It's the same mistake many economists make, believing that responses are cast in concrete, and what happened last time will repeat. Most (private) economic agents are more flexible, and attempt to align their actons with events they wish to see happen, or when without control, to protect themselves against possible risks. Their actions will thus differ over a period of time because they perceive risks differently.

The mood of the economy is changing, from a period of high growth to a leveling of economic activity. If we respond intelligently to this slowing, we can maintain a healthy economy that will serve us well. If we refuse to recognize the necessity for the slowing, as we appear to be bent, then excessive development of structures not required will require major adjustments in the future. It is a time of long leads and lags, and a major change of trends in the economy. Let's hope we can act now to stabilize the '80s.

What we are concerned with here is the market and its perception of the economy, and not the economy itself. It does appear, from the vacillations of the market, that there is a great deal of uncertainty affecting the general level of prices. In such times of uncertainty, the wise investment decision is to rely on fundamental value of efficiently operating assets to protect against downside risk. The price level is, in fact, being repressed toward a more basic valuaton of securities. The high flying days of the '60s appear to be gone, much to the relief of most legitimate investors. However, the emotional content of the market is still high, and it seems that the new mood of the market is one of pessimism, unfortunately, rather than a return to fundamental value.

Chapter 7

Ratios

Quickie guides to further study.

There are some ratios and relationships that are used to evaluate the market and its specific issues, and it seems worthwhile to briefly review their efficacy in valuation. They are pervasive in the literature and information of the market, and their ready availability can be used to the advantage of the individual investor. They can be used like bookends, or budget variance limits, to bracket an area of interest, and therefore reduce the number of considerations in a wide market to a reasonable number. None of these brackets can be stated as absolutes, for the market is too variable for that. They can be stated as relative measures of where a company stands in its own progress and what valuation the market has placed on this standing. The market variability might affect the entire width of the market, as would be the case in changing moods of the investors. The variability might alternately be reflected in one segment of the market, more or less, as would be the case during the general development level of a bull or bear market. **95**

It might be wise to recall our purpose. It is to minimize the risks in investing in a speculative medium. Whether the risks come from the changing moods, from the general cyclical reaction of the market, of from the variances of the different segments of the market, they can be minimized by recognizing the status of the market at a particular time. It is this action by the investor that can reduce the risks of investing from the combination of market and business risk to a more measurable business risk alone. We are looking primarily for a reasonable return on the investment with some predictable stability. Investing, then, becomes an economic decision, at least somewhat apart from the emotional control of the financial market. We are interested primarily in fundamental value in an investment. Once we gain that, should the market action add value to our investments, it is a plus to our objectives of capital maintenance and a minimum reasonable return, given current economic circumstances.

Numerous attempts have been made to define a mathematical formula for market valuation. One such study, completed in the highflying '60s, proposed a P/E of 15 for a company with an expected growth of 3.5% per year. Today, with the average of the top 3300 issues selling at a P/E of under 8, this quantitative study becomes ludicrous. Not only have the cyclical reactions of the market carried us toward a relative low, but the general mood of the market has dramatically changed. Today, at least for the short term, dividends have become a more important part of valuation, and a high inflation premium is demanded. It is not that the studies are of no value, but that events are continually changing, and only a relative measure of value is of advantage over an extended period of time. Even such a relative measure may be outmoded by changing structure over the long term.

Ratios can be highly misleading if used by themselves without reference to the underlying figures. A high P/E ratio might result from a temporary lapse in earnings, while the market continues its previous valuation of that issue. A variance in the P/E ratio might also result from market consideration of specific accounting rules used by the firm, or one-time writeoffs. A ratio such as P/E can only be properly understood by knowledge of the industry, and study of historical valuation, along with detailed knowledge of the capabilities of the firm. Used in general to determine the level of development of the market, and to understand the place of the firm in the segments of the market, it can be used effectively as a first level of review.

Over the past few decades, analysts have developed a method of viewing the market that can be of use to us here. It encompasses a division of return in the market into various components that are easier to deal with individually. Return, as used here, is the combination of dividends (including stock), capital gains (whether realized or not), and other distributions. Over a period of time, a certain return can be measured for the market as a whole, or some segment of it. Then a portfolio, or a particular stock, can be measured against this return, to measure the relative value of the investment in the market. The returns of the portfolio or stock can be either lesser or greater than those of the market, or segment, in general, and the values will be either negative or positive.

The return on the portfolio or stock is typically divided into three components. The first is the Alpha, representing a basic return. It has been used in two forms, one representing the variance from the market return (that is, the return on the issue equals the market return plus or minus the Alpha), and the other the variance above or below the return on a riskless asset (such as Treasury Bills). The variance from the market return is generally easier to comprehend, and is considered here, though the change in general relationships to ratios and their effectiveness in valuation is insignificant. The Alpha is thus a measure of the return premium gained by superior forecasting of security prices. Theoretically, a random selection of issues would yield an Alpha of zero, and effective investments would yield a positive Alpha.

The second component is the Beta, and represents the extent to which the particular issue (or portfolio) reflects the movements of the general market above or below the level of the Alpha. A Beta of 1 means that the issue moves in conjunction with the market, and a market movement of +10% is reflected by a +10% move in the price of the issue. Similarly, a Beta of 2 means that a +10% market move will result in a +20% move in the issue, and a Beta of zero indicates no change in the issue price, even though the market makes strong moves. The third component measures the unique return associated with a particular issue, typically computed as a residual from the other two measures, thus usually referred to as the Residual. Its expected value is zero.

Since variability is typically used to measure risk in the market, the Beta is typicaly used as a value of risk for a particular stock, and the Alpha can then be computed as a risk adjusted return for the stock. An investor would desire a high (positive) Alpha, and the Beta value would be determined by future moves of the market, as envisioned by the investor. In a bull market, a high Beta would be desirable and the rising market would add leverage to the movements of the stock (with a Beta over 1). In a declining market, a low Beta would be a defensive mechanism.

While these measures are nice mathematical indexes, they sometimes lead the investor to believe they have mathematical precision. In computation they do, but they can be highly imprecise indicators of the status of a particular issue. A company might have a high Beta because it has been in a steady uptrend. If the Beta was measured over perhaps a three year period, and that period consisted primarily of a bull market, the high Beta might result. The same stock, experiencing a general uptrend in price resulting from a technological breakthrough, could have a low Beta (perhaps negative) if measured during a general bear market. This word of caution appears necessary when applying such a general measure to a specific issue.

There are particular relationships that exist between the Betas and the Alphas, and some generally used ratios. Not only are these generally reinforcing when used in selecting a stock for a particular set of circumstances in the market, but they are some indication of the segment of the market in which an investor might be interested at a particular time. Consider for example, the relationship shown in Figure 7-1, where the Beta is related to the P/E. The P/E is used for illustration because it is probably the most used ratio, and it has been shown to be the most effective in stock selection. Perhaps that is begging the question, because if it is the most used, the market should show the greatest response to its movement. If only for that reason, it is of value. You can see that a low P/E is associated with a high Beta. That is what might be expected. The low P/E company is typically the smaller and/or less stable company, that the market has discounted in price, perhaps because of the volatility of its income stream, or for other internal or external reasons.

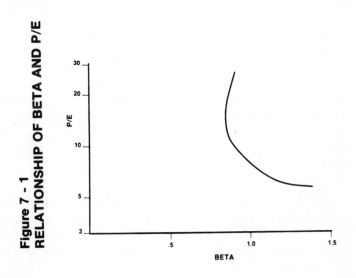

Figure 7 - 1
RELATIONSHIP OF BETA AND P/E

At the other end of the relationship, the Beta again becomes higher in relation to higher P/E's. These are the growth companies that have outperformed the market in general, and have thus been assigned a high price by investors looking for growth. Included in this portion of the relationship might also be some typically low P/E companies that have lost earnings and are resting on a fundamental base, particularly at a low in the business cycle. Both measures, the Beta and the P/E rankings consist of a mingling of diverse stocks from diverse industries. However, the general relationship of higher Betas associated with low P/Es is obvious, and logical. If an investor were assured (reasonably) of a coming bull market, and wanted to participate fully with a high Beta stock, he would logically find that selection in a low P/E stock. It might be noted that this is a characteristic that might change its slope over time, but the general form will not change too much. An investor seeking a defensive posture will do best in the refuge of the center of the market segment, in general, with the lowest Beta available.

The payout ratio is also consistently related to the Beta, with a high Beta found in companies with both a particularly high and a particularly low payout ratio. Recall that the Beta is a measure of risk, and either a high or low payout ratio might be suspect. Too high a payout might indicate reduced opportunities for the company, with nothing left for the use of the earnings except dividends, where the investors could use the funds for better return in other parts of the market. This portion of the relationship is often subverted by management unwilling to yield the funds, even though new opportunities have not been developed.

At the other extreme of the relationship, a company with a particularly low payout may have the exceptional opportunities that entice the market to assign a high price to the issue, and thus force a movement in price far faster than the movement of the market in general. Theoretically, given an adequate return on capital, the growth rate of the firm is inversely related to the payout ratio. (Given the limiting actions of management, this may or may not be true). But the higher growth rate and extensions of operations carry with it increasing risk. This risk is represented by the Beta, but it may also represent market movement resulting from successful operations that in fact reduce the risk of the stock. Fast growth of the company and its attendant price may or may not be risky. The high Beta is more conclusive the longer the time period over which it is measured.

High Betas are associated with low total invested capital, and low Betas are associated with large capital. This merely confirms the volatility (and riskiness) of the smaller companies. The relationship is not completely linear across the market, though. It appears that the lower end of the market (in terms of capital) bears a strong relationship to high Betas, but in the central and upper market, this relationship is maintained relatively level. What that means is that there is little to be gained in risk reduction, as measured by the Beta, by investing in the "larger" firms of the market. Except for the lower extremes, the risk is somewhat constant.

The same general type of relationship exists between the Betas and return on capital, that is, low rates of return are associated with high Betas (risk). The relationship is more linear, though, with a constantly decreasing slope. At the upper end of this relationship is the risk averter who believes that superior returns (in terms of the risk-return relationship) are available from companies with high rates of earnings. However, it might be noted that during a bull market, companies with lower rates of return could yield better market returns, in terms of price appreciation.

There is an argument in finance that debt/equity ratios do not affect market valuation. In spite of that argument, all studies have shown that companies with low debt/capital ratios have low Betas, and companies with high debt/capital ratios have high Betas. It seems that the market still considers high potential leverage as a risk, as well as the basis for higher prices on the security in times of rising markets. But then, we already knew that.

Relationships to the Alpha are not so readily available. Not only is the Alpha less readily understood, but results have been less informative about a specific security, even when applied by capable analysts. It may be that the Alpha is a depth of thinking beyond the capability of the typical trader and investor, in today's market.

Figure 7 - 2
RELATIONSHIP OF ALPHA AND PAYOUT RATIO

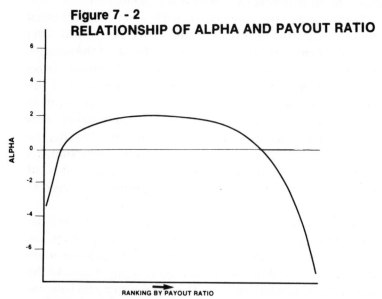

One reasonably consistent relationship is shown in Figure 7-2. Individual companies have been ranked by their payout ratio, with the largest payout to the right. It can be noted that both extremes of the market yield an inadequate return, in relation to the risk assumed. At the upper end, too high a payout indicates declining opportunities (or declining revenues and an attempt to maintain a dividend). The dividend is typically high, but the issue is not of investment value because of the high risk that must be assumed. At the lower end, the return is low and the risk is high as measured by the Beta. This may be the growth company that has high price changes in relation to the market, and this carries a high Beta. The shortcoming of the Beta as a measure of risk, and the shortcoming of the definition of risk as synonymous with volatility is obvious. However, before we too quickly dismiss the picture of Figure 7-2, the dangers of a high P/E stock should be remembered in the light of the recent strong bear market.

A very strong relation to the Alpha is found in the rate of return, particularly in the high rate of return end of the relationship. As any investor might have told us, this indicates that superior quality overall market returns are gained from companies with high rates of return on capital. Efficiently operating assets is always the basis of the market, even though that view is often temporarily lost in the emotional control of the market. It is a basic that should always be the first requirement in selecting an investment.

Note that throughout all of the above relationships, the high risk is associated with the extremes of the market. Sometimes it can yield an exceptional overall return, but more often, the risk attendant to the extremes in inadequately compensated. That means that the typical attempt to outperform the central market must assume inordinate risk, and, in the long run, the total return will be inadequate to maintain capital and still match return of a less risky approach to the market. The central market is still wide, with a strong slope, and numerous variations are available to trader, speculator, or investor. For the (long term) investor, it is usually the only appropriate portion of the market for his activities.

Of course, in all these measures, a large portion of the market has been thrown together, without consideration for industry, or peculiarities of individual issues. The combined view may be instructive, however, of the general action of the market, and the reasons for that action. The ratios cannot be a substitute for detailed attention to the individual issue, but they may shortcut the process of finding the issue desired. That particular issue, and its associated ratios and characteristics, will vary with the timing of the market. A different type of issue will be appropriate in times of rising markets, or relative stability, for example. No one issue perfectly fits a time in the market, and yet an issue may reasonably fit more than one time. The stocks of the market are wide enough that they form a continuum in most characteristics, and offer the investor multiple methods of reaching an investment goal.

Part III

The Particular Stock

No matter how well an investor might understand the market and the moods that surround it, the particular issue is the vehicle in which the investment must be made. The final objective has always been to make money, and to make as much as possible while assuming a limited risk commensurate with the position of the particular investor.

Just as the market is constantly changing, to the point of excessive volatility, so are the individual issues. Any one issue typically varies in price between at least fifteen and fifty percent in each year, and in special situations or during strong market changes vary much more. The particular issue may be less important than selecting an issue with the appropriate volatility for the particular times. Even after the right class of issue is selected, the proper timing is paramount, and this requires exceptional knowledge about the particular issue. It is thus better to know a great deal about a few issues or even a single issue, than to concentrate on too many issues so that depth of knowledge might be lost.

Starting with the A's in the *Wall Street Journal* is hardly an effective method for stock selection. It is necessary to select a stock about which information can be regularly obtained. The best way to be sure of continuing information is to select stocks that have some proximity to the investor. This proximity might be geographical, in which local stocks are the point of concentration. Continuing information will usually be available regularly in local publications, and the investor has the opportunity to attend annual meetings, and keep in contact with the company by phone when unusual situations arise. The investor can also select stocks from his technical specialty. This is, after all, his special fund of information, and he is usually aware of new and continuing developments in that particular field.

Whatever the method used to obtain current information, the company selected should be an efficiently operating and well managed one. The investor then has a gauge of fundamental value from the regular and increasing stream of earnings. This can provide a basic market value that protects the investor's capital from depreciation, while providing the possibilities of capital gain. Proper valuation of an issue is important so that the investor does not purchase a stock after the market has overpriced it. At any one time, there are good fundamental values available in the market. The market price of an issue is always right, but only at that time, and an investor must always buy future value.

Chapter 8

Proximity

*Local areas or personal specialty for
depth of knowledge.*

There is a precept of management that joins
responsibility with authority over a situation. It is an
impossible situation to have responsibility for
accomplishment of a given task unless one has the authority
to take action to see that the task is undertaken properly and
with direction. There is a correlary to this in financial
management; that no investment (responsibility) should be
undertaken without the ability to control that investment.

Of course, as a stockholder, particularly a small one, one
does not typically control the company whose stock is held.
What can be controlled is the investment, for the investor
alone can make the decision to buy or hold the stock. What is
needed to make this decision is accurate and timely
information. Most public companies work hard at providing
this information, but the markets are simply too big for an
investor to have full information at his fingertips for more
than a few investments at a time. When the investor
becomes interested in a potential stock, he can turn to the

investment advisories that summarize 3000 stocks, but all that he can get is summary information. **It is always far better in the market to have in-depth information about a very few investments, than to have information about all stocks in general.**

The best source of information about stocks always comes from one's own backyard, and from the investor's current sources of business information. To review a potential investment should take minimal exertion on the part of the investor. If investment review is difficult and time-consuming, the job will not be adequately or regularly accomplished. The best source of information is the local newspaper (or it should be), and perhaps the local legal newspaper or "daily record". While their depth of coverage is always inadequate, access to the annual report and 10K* of a firm, attendance of the annual meeting, and a contact inside the company can give the investor more information about the firm than the average securities analyst possesses. The newspaper keeps him current, and depth of problem areas can be ferreted out from the 10K and by intelligent questioning of the company officers or other contacts available to him.

The newspaper that the investor reads may not be the daily general newspaper for the general area. If he spends a few hours every weekend reading *Communications News,* then that may be his newspaper. A satellite engineer with current knowledge of the industry would have been blind not to have seen the success of the radio equipment manufacturers that jumped on the bandwagon of satellite communications in the early and mid '70s. Unfortunately, many engineers who spent their 50 hours a week studying the industry were cajoled into putting their capital into a steel company, for example, that didn't show half the promise of companies with which they were intimately familiar. It might be noted that fundamentals and industry analysis are never adequate by themselves, but they are basics from which we must start. The basic requirement for any investment is efficiently operating assets, even though profit is primarily attained from the market evaluation of those assets.

If you don't have a specialty industry with which you have close and continuous contact, then the best specialty that you can have is local area stocks. Almost everyone is close enough to a major city that has adequate major stock exchange and other listed securities from which to select a portfolio. If you select this geographical proximity for your stock selections, it is possible to keep in constant touch with a particular company. Don't be afraid to call the company directly and request information. Most large firms have an investor relations function, and in small firms you can usually gain direct access to the financial officer or the president. A personal call daily or even weekly might be met with great resistance, but a quarterly call to present intelligent queries about specific developments can yield you surprisingly cordial treatment and informative gems.

These officers are accustomed to being questioned by current and prospective stockholders, security analysts, and the media. However, there are certain disclosure rules by which they must abide. The most important of these is that in general, information concerning the firm must be readily available to all potential investors at the same time. That means simply that you should not expect to receive confidences from any officer, for example, concerning some

---

*The 10K is a report to the SEC of company business by product line, and other detailed information. Copies are usually provided by companies to potential investors without charge. However, an increasingly large number of companies are incorporating important information from the 10K into their annual report, so that the 10K becomes unnecessary for detailed review of company operations. Remember that it is expensive for a company to provide these reports, and requests for information should be limited to definite needs.

anticipated future event ("our earnings forecast is being revised"), or particular management move ("we're discussing merger"). The information you do receive will keep you up-to-date on what is generally available to the market.

Along the same line, the best annual information you can obtain is that presented at the annual meeting. It is also the best place to have an opportunity to question management with the expectation of receiving qualified replies. The information presented here is considered available to the market, since the meeting is open to the public. This means that the president or financial officer can speculate on what might happen in case of a particular event, and it is this information that can give the best insight to characteristics of that particular firm. Of course, there are certain secrecy requirements that the officers may invoke to protect the firm from competition, and they will not directly answer all questions. Nevertheless, this meeting is the most informative source available to investors. Certainly, you cannot attend the meeting of that little firm three thousand miles away that you were considering as a buy, and it is unlikely that their annual meeting notes will be picked up by the financial press. Stick with a company about which you can obtain maximum information. Most often that is the company in your own back yard, and for the average investor that means physical proximity.

I usually recommend that an investor review two specialty areas as a long range investment review. One is the specialty of the individual and the other is the physical proximity of local stocks. In certain special cases, this will not offer adequate diversity on which to build a portfolio, and the area of physical proximity must be extended. An investor might start with the general metropolitan area, then extend to the statistical area (generall five or six counties), then extend to a portion of the state. I can't think of a single instance in which this would not offer an adequately diversified portfolio. An investor can usually follow about twenty stocks, but this varies with the amount of time available, and the interest of the investor, as well as the size of the portfolio. Following twenty stocks will allow about ten in a specialty field and ten in the local area. That is adequate to fully cover the depth of the market by allowing for New York Stock Exchange (NYSE) and American Stock Exchange (ASE) stocks as well as including some Over-theCounter (OTC) stocks. This depth of coverage is of primary importance, as discussed in Chapter 4.

How can you find these stocks? The best source is the local newspaper and other information sources pertaining to a specialty. The next best source of guidance is the broker and market maker. If an OTC stock is headquartered and traded locally, there is probably a local market maker. The best place to find him is through the financial office of the firm itself, but once you have found a legitimate and knowledgable broker, he will lead you to other stocks. A sovrce of information for local stocks is not always a local brokerage firm. Many times a national brokerage firm wil have the personnel and capabilities to be the best source of information about local stocks.

However, don't rely too heavily on any local source. It might also be said not to rely too heavily on any source. The market can make horrendous mistakes in its stupidity. I recall the consternation of the chief financial officer of one firm for which I worked. The stock was going up, and seemed about to double in price in a week. It was listed on ASE and the phone rang all day long with people trying to find out what was happening. We simply didn't know. In fact, the firm was doing poorly on one of its major contracts, and was a definite sell. What we later found was that another company with a name similar to ours had made a breakthrough, and their stock also doubled in a week. Our stock returned to normal in a few weeks, but there must have been some sorrowful investors (and brokers) when they found what they had really purchased.

The best source of local information is always the local

library. If you are lucky, you will find a well organized section of financial information and it will include specific informaton on local companies. More likely than not, however, you will find some scattered information on a few selected local companies and little else. If this is the case in your city, ask each of the companies that you contact for information to also forward the same information to the local library and to put the library on their mailing list. Next time that you need updated information, it will be available. Many libraries simply don't have the funds to maintain an active file on local companies, because budget cuts have severly limited their staffs. Recommend to the library that they establish a simple alphabetical file of annual reports and other information relating to specific companies. It is usually a short task for an investor to go through such a file and quickly obtain information of importance to his particular need.

Most chamber of commerce organizations publish some directory of businesses in their particular area. Many of these directories contain keys to publically traded companies. If they do not, often the chamber office will assist you in selecting the companies in which you may be interested. The list that you obtain in this way will give you market depth far beyond the usually abbreviated listings in the newspaper. However, it is not recommended that you invest in any company on which you cannot obtain regular information. If your broker has to go to his "pink" sheets for a quote or there is no activity in a stock, it is not a potential investment unless you have a particular tie or contact with the stock.

The best source of information is to be a participant in the company. It is the enviable position of having access to insider information without being an "insider". The position will not yield you sure profits, for the market price is seldom related to value or efficiency of assets, directly. However, a financial history of a particular company combined with in-depth knowledge in the profit and loss can give you an early insight to future market moves. I knew one investor who worked for a publicly traded "dog" and had put in extensive time researching the financial history of the company and its place in the market. The stock had a typical median cycle (4+ years) low price of 1 and a typical high of 5. It was in a cyclical industry, and the stock retained its volatility in spite of earnings reports. When the stock became underpriced, this investor loaded up, regardless of the latest profit report. When the stock became overpriced, he sold it, and salted the money away while the decline ensued. Over a twenty year period this individual became rich from his trading. In the later years, he began to participate in the shorter term (19 weeks) cycles of the stock. He couldn't afford to retire, even though he no longer needed the money from his job. He had diversified his investments in later years by studying the companies that worked with his, either as a supplier or as a customer. It was legend in the business the grilling that this investor would give an executive from another company when he got the opportunity. This investor had one secret, and it was that **he never told anyone what he was doing,** either in the company or out of it. He used multiple brokers, and never sold through a broker from whom he had bought. Working the market as he did is a game in which only a very small percent can participate. When the specialty is as narrow as his, secrecy is even more important.

If you are dealing with a company on one of the major exchanges, the leads and lags of the business cycle to the market cycle will be rather obvious and somewhat easy to ascertain. However, when you begin to deal with OTC companies that are located primarily in one particular area, the leads and lags, and even the business cycle may differ from those that are developing nationally. This information must be followed carefully, for the difference in timing can mean the success or failure of your investment program. Be aware that there may be differences, and they will not be too difficult to ascertain, and in most cases they will be small.

There is a more difficult factor to ascertain in a given

area, and its difficulty is caused by its obvious character. There will be different moods of investor climate at different points of time. For example, the northeast is currently suffering an exodus of business, and it is likely that the trend will continue for some time. This has not affected the major national firms headquartered in the area, but some of the smaller companies that have national exposure have been severly underpriced by the market. The risk really wasn't that great, but the market always overreacts. The result of the undervaluation has been a rash of mergers and takeovers in these middle market stocks. The stocks that are primarily local in nature (not large enough to receive national exposure) have fared much better in the marketplace so that inadequate recognition has been given to their risk component, at least in relation to the national middle market stocks. The stocks that hold the best long range investment potential should be obvious, but timing of the buy is highly critical. It is part of investing that the larger the potential gain, the more important is timing. A good buy doesn't last on the market for long.

A word of warning on the use of proximity. Industries tend to group together. Where one firm operates and capable personnel are available, it is likely that other firms in the same or related industries will start. If your specialty is also the primary industry of the area, beware of the risk of a single industry. Perhaps you should seek some diversification in some way.

That need not be a real limitation. I know of no area of any size where industry is not sufficiently diversified to offer an efficient portfolio with adequate risk minimization. The important thing is for the investor to have timely and accurate information available to him in some usable form. The services are nice, quick, easy reference material that a million other investors will see. If you want to feel safe by doing what all the other investors are doing, this book will probably be of little value to you anyway. If you want to develop you own information for independent decisions, the

suggestions on the use of proximity should be highly
rewarding.

Chapter 9

Fundamental Value

*Efficiently operating assets
as a first requirement.*

There are two objectives in mind when selecting an investment. The first is capital maintenance, protecting the invested capital by minimizing downside potential for prices. The second is profitability, using the tendency of the stock price to increase. The first is accomplished in part by selecting a profitable company that has efficiently operating assets, and inherent characteristics that tend toward profit improvement. However, the market seldom directly reflects the profitability of a company. It is possible to invest in a highly profitable situation, only to see the market value of that investment decrease at the same time that it is becoming even more profitable. Some of this phenomenon has to do with timing, some with the preferences of the market at a particular time, and some with the oeration of the "auction" market.

It is basic to protecting the invested capital that the company in which the investment is being made be a profitable entity. (In speculative investments such as a start-up situation, this might mean some promise of profitability.) In such a case, it means an efficiently operating company in a good market position, in the position of working toward its most efficient operating point. In other words, the fundamental value of the company must be high or increasing. The purpose then, in selecting an investment, is to minimize the implicit risk component, while looking for a situation in which the market has placed a higher risk value on the particular investment, by lowering the price below fundamental value.

Figure 9 - 1
CONCEPT OF VALUATION

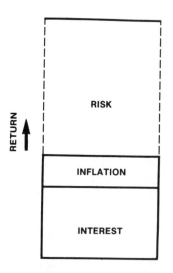

The return on any investment can be broken down into three components. These are shown in Figure 9-1, where the return consists of interest, an inflation component, and a risk factor. How the risk of a particular company is envisioned by the market will determine what value will be placed on those assets and the return that they will generate.

Quite a few studies have been made to determine what the pure (riskless) return has been. By most studies, this interest for the use of money has averaged betwen 2 ½ to 3% in the twentieth century.* This is the return that an investor would receive if he placed money in an investment in which he could be assured of being repaid, usually approximated in U.S. government securities. More money could always be printed to pay the investment when due, but the inflationary effects of such a move prevent this type of investment from being entirely riskless.

---

* In the early '70s, a Morgan Guaranty study yielded a figure of 3.13% for Europe and America. This was close to agreement with a much referenced study in the late '50s by Sir John Hicks of the Radcliff Committee in Britain. That study produced a figure of 3% for the European countries. Other studies of the '60s produced figures in the range of 2.6% to 3.2%. The consensus of opinion has been a return of just under 3%. However, two recent studies have yielded different results. Ibbotson and Sinquefield in *Stocks, Bonds, Bills, and Inflation: The Past (1926-1976) and the Future (1977-2000)*, Financial Analysts Research Foundation, 1977 found a return on U.S. Treasury Bills of 2.4% for the fifty years, but an inflation rate of 2.3%, yielding an inflaton adjusted rate of .1%. Fisher and Lorie in *A Half Century of Returns on Stocks and Bonds,* The University of Chicago, 1977 found a rate of return on short-term U.S. Treasury Securities of 3.0% for the same fifty year period. The rate of return deflated by the Consumer Price Index is .7%. (Both studies used the same computer stored data base.) They both indicate that the pure rate of interest has failed to keep up with inflation over the last thirty years, so that the real rate of return may be close to zero. In the longer term, the basic 3.0% rate still appears to be near the considered requirement of investors.

Of course, the dollars in which an investor would be repaid might not be as valuable as those in which he had invested. The return would have to be adequate to compensate the investor for taking this chance. It would have to contain an inflation component. Note that this part of the return is a return of capital. Many investors who would stoutly follow the rule of never touching their basic capital make the mistake of considering this component as a return on their investment, which it is not. If an investor wishes to maintain his capital, his component should be reinvested. Of course, it will be different for different types of investments. This diversity is due to the timing of their payoff, and the anticipation of the market for inflatoin during that time period.

The last component, return for assumed risk, might vary in value from essentially zero to any upwards value. It has been shown, in fact, that in the end of the market of minimum risk, this factor may even be negative. Risk averters may select a conservative investment that has inadequate return to account for inflation. By turning to these investments as a hedge against risk, the investor is actually allowing his capital account to decrease over time. Such riskless investments are important for the market, but for the individual investor they should be only a short term vehicle for their capital.

Market valuation of the risk component has never been adequately measured to allow a precise understanding of it. Certainly, it has varied over time, and has most often been defined as being measured by the volatility of an investment. At low levels of risk, a particular return is reasonably assured, within some narrow limits of variability. In a more risky investment, the return is more variable, and the posibility of not receiving an adequate return is more likely. The assets are thus valued lower than if the investment's return could be assured.

'Of course, variability in itself is not necessarily bad. Only if the variability would reduce the return would it harm our investment.If the variability would tend to increase the return on the investment, the value of the assets in the future should rise. This is one of the major factors that an investor should seek out in the market. It is a situation in which the market has undervalued an asset because of its variability, while in fact that variability is surrounded in circumstances which will tend to increase the potential return from that investment. Of course, the fundamental value of the firm must be above that assigned it by the market, and the characteristics of the firm must be such that, in time and position, the potential return is skewed upward.

We will find situations in which the market has undervalued a particular investment. Usually this is in a period of overreaction (as discussed in Chapter 1.), and all assets of a particular class may be undervalued. In such a circumstance, the company with the most efficiently operating assets, and with the highest topside potential in return will make the best investment within that class. It is terribly important to understand the market and its vagaries when attempting to invest within that market. The entire approach of this method of investing is oriented toward the use of market volatility. However, no investment should even be undertaken without basic values behind that investment. Any stock market investment begins with a sound company with efficiently operating assets.

It is interesting to note where the market stands with respect to the concept of valuation mentioned above. If the 3% return is accepted as the long term rate of interest allocated by the market for the use of capital, the current valuation would be built up as shown in Figure 9-2. The current long term inflation rate is figured to be running at about 6% per year. In fact, the actual inflation rate is closer to 8% in terms of buying power from a salary or fixed income. This is because the inflaton rate does not contain a tax component. As a salary increases to maintain purchasing power in times of inflation, the progressive tax system takes a larger marginal percent of that salary for taxes.

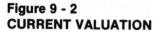

Figure 9 - 2
CURRENT VALUATION

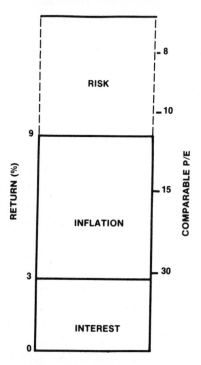

However, accepting the 6% figure for the moment and adding it to the interest indicates a minimum return of about 9% for a riskless investment. In early 1977, before the market began its current bear market, stocks were selling at an average price/earnings ratio (P/E) of about 10, giving an average earnings yield of about 10%. It should not be too surprising that the market moved downward. With an average P/E of just over 7, the return from earnings is closer to 14%, giving a risk factor of about 5%, in mid 1978. If you feel that inflation is becoming a fixed part of governmental fiscal policy (as I do), then in the intermediate term, it might be anticipated that interst rates will rise, and to maintain the risk component, P/E's will decline even more. Certainly, an announced $60 billion deficit for the 1979 fiscal year of the federal government does not indicate any intention to attempt to control the inflation that is induced by fiscal policy.

So, as a basic requirement for investing, we want to find a good company in a good environment. A good company is one that is meeting a need of the market, with an evident understanding of the potential changes in that market. The market itself may be expanding, perhaps as a result of use of new technology, or the application of existing technology to new uses. However, the application of existing technology may occur in a sphere of high competition, or that competition may be developed from that new application. One recent example was the explosion in sales of citizens' band radios. Certainly the technology existed, and the race to capture an expanding market left behind the dead (in bankruptcy) and the wounded (in which a substantial investment became a one-time writeoff). Such markets are a type of fad, even though the long term market may be increasing. The response to the market is an overreaction, without adequate consideration of the long range consequences. Thus, a "hot" market is often hazardous.

A company may also be gaining an expanding market by increasing its capture of an existing, but stable market. That may indicate a strong management, which is the most important ingredient to long range profitability. However, if the company is moving away from its efficient operating point, in the long run a move to capture additional market share will be bad for the company and its profitability.* There is usually an inherent position in the market that is dictated by the characteristics of a particular firm. These characteristics are not solely a limiting factor, for it is a measure of capable management that they can shift this

---

*For example, see the discussion of this point in "Part III Characteristics of the Firm" of my book, *Management of the Firm,* Concept Publishing, 1977.

operating point over time to meet the needs of the market. An example happens often in high technology companies. Most high technology markets start with high quality (and price), fulfilling a small segment of market demand, or a new demand for which the technology was developed to serve. Thus the company is established for and has experience in servicing a small volume market in which service of the firm is to the individual customer, and quality is paramount. Often, however, this technology is developed over time to service a mass market at low cost. Some recent examples are the calculator and digital watches, and a current example is the solar cells, once produced for satellites and now being used in home heating systems. If management is incapable of shifting its operating curve, the firm will either incur serious financial difficulties or merely lose the market. (There are, of course, many other reasons for withdrawing from a market in which a company may have had a strong foothold.)

There are, of course, growth industries and special situations that appear to be highly desirable investments. If the growth is real, they may be desirable, but the firm that is to be the vehicle to these opportunities must be strong in its position, relative to those same opportunities. At an early stage of such opportunities, the concept of management, as well as its ability to direct the firm toward its proper place in the market, is of highest importance. Many firms have had the opportunities, but few have had the capability to take advantage of them adequately.

Most firms have some method of considering the investment opportunities that are available to the firm. The simplest of these is a ranking of the projects by their estimated rate of return, from the highest to the lowest. A firm would accept the projects with the highest rates of return, down to a point of limited capital availability, or a higher available rate in alternate uses for the capital. If it appears to the firm that their investors may have opportunities for higher return in other segments of the market, the decision might be made to increase dividends, and thus allow the investors to seek these other returns. (The tax situation must be considered by the firm, weighing the double tax on dividends against capital gains potential.) A particularly high payout in dividends, in relation to the industry, might be a sign of diminishing opportunities for the company, and a particularly low payout might indicate numerous other opportunities at high rates of return for the firm. Many other factors affect the dividend decision, and a particularly low dividend payout can harm the market for the security, but this measure may be some indication of the status of the firm in the market.

Some investors use book value as an indication of the intrinsic value of a stock. It may be of some value to consider this factor, but most firms have been established long enough so that the relationship of book to market value is vague at best. It is much more important to consider the efficiency of recent additions to capital. Retained earnings should contribute to an increasing rate of return on invested capital. Consideration of the marginal efficiency of recently contributed capital can thus give some insight to the market opportunities available to the firm. A management that is investing its earnings in opportunities that offer less return than available in alternate investments (i.e., available to the investor through a dividend payout) may be trying to preserve the position of the firm in the market at the expense of the investor's long term interests.

Many instances could probably be found of successful investments that were not based on efficient and profitable business operations. Most of these, however, would be found to have rested on investor expectations of profitable business operations. Without efficiently operating assets, and a good market position, the downside risk of a firm becomes considerable, and thus the security becomes a poor investment vehicle.

Part III / The Particular Stock

Chapter 10

Valuation

The market is always right.

The key to successful investing in any medium is proper valuation of the particular investment. The "correct" valuation is not what a particular investor may think the security may be worth. It is what the market decides is a proper value within some specified time frame. The market may think little of an investment today, and the individual investor may think the market is wrong: that is, that the investment is undervalued. Should the investor decide to invest in that security, he can only be proven right about the future potential of the value if tomorrow the market decides to value that security higher than it did previously.

There are many capital losers in the market who were "right" about an investment. The firm may have become profitable and prospered, but if the market did not recognize its newfound success, or still considered risk (volatility) as too high a probability, the investor has not been right about the investment, yet. The time may come, and it may be worthwhile to continue the investment in the security, but each new time frame must bring a new evaluation of that particular security. The moods of the market change, particularly with time, and what may have been a proper valuation yesterday may be completely out of line with today's market. Valuation formulas cannot give a level of prices. Prices can only be stated for today, and in relation to the rest of the market.

The problem of time is considered in Part II, but here we will consider the relation of a particular investment to the rest of the market. If we view a firm as some combination of assets operating at some degree of efficiency, then we can ask: at what price are the earnings adequate to support that price in today's (or tomorrow's) market? The use of those earnings may have a large effect on valuation depending on whether they are paid out as dividends or reinvested, and how they are reinvested. These actions will be evaluated differently by different segments of the market.

While there is a continuum of attitudes and needs in the market, it is convenient and instructive to divide the market into three segments. There is a central market around which most of the activity of valuation occurs. It usually represents a technical valuation of risk in the market and the associated return. When there is high risk, as perceived by the market (usually in terms of volatility of profits) a higher return will be demanded by the market for investing in those assets. This is accomplished by marking down the price, so that the existing return provides a rate of return superior to more stable profits. This discounting exists in the central market in a mathematical relationship that is highly precise, given a certain level of the market.

At the upper end of the market is a group of investors who do not wish to accept the risk of the market. They are the risk averters who seek out stable earnings streams and pay a high price to obtain the assets that produce them. They typically seek out larger firms, so that there is diversification with each investment, as well as within the portfolio. Random losses, such as floods, fire, etc., can be somewhat obscured in overall return by such dual diversification. Most of all, they seek stability of earnings, associated with an increasing earnings stream. In short, they seek a market position that allows efficient use of available capital derived from retained earnings.

At the other end of the market are the risk takers, the gamblers in the market. They will accept a (potentially) unstable earnings stream, if the market has discounted it adequately. They will bet on a particular situation being successful; that is, that the earnings stream will continue or increase, and they will risk loss of capital because the return will be exceptional. On the average, the return to this group, based on the number of successes, is very small in relation to the risk assumed. Often, the average level of return is less than the average level of return received by the risk averters at the other extreme of the market. But individually, there are extreme returns for the successful risk takers, and there never seems to be a paucity of investors at this end of the market.

Any price in the market is a function of supply and demand (in the long run). A particular investor does not exist in a particular segment of the market. He visits that segment, as conditions of the market dictate. Thus, each segment of the market has different supply and demand functions as conditions change. The supply side of the relationship is determined by the business conditions, and the stage of the business cycle(s). A dog yesterday may have strong probabilities of future earnings today, because of changing conditions in business structure, consumer demand, government control, etc. At the same time, companies lose the future potential of their earnings stream for the same reasons. Future profitability potential may as well be effected by events internal to the company or from within the industry.

The segments of the market are shown in Figure 10-1. The companies of the market have been ranked according to their price/earnings (P/E) ratio that exists at a particular

Figure 10 - 1
SEGMENTS OF THE MARKET

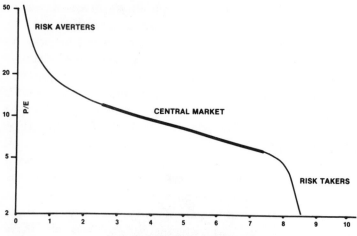

Figure 10 - 1 SEGMENTS OF THE MARKET

time. The high P/Es represent the risk averters, and the low P/Es the market discount given to induce the risk takers. The central market is essentially a straight line (on ratio paper), in which a certain slope represents the mood and stage of development of the market at a particular time. A proper valuation of a security will depend on the mood of the market as represented by the (1) slope of the central market and (2) the extent of the extremes (risk aversion and risk taking) of the market. Determining these two attributes of the market could be a reasonably easy technical function, except that an adequate evaluation must consider what is (3) the proper level of the central market, and what will be (4) the position of the above three factors tomorrow.

The demand side of the relationship is developed within the market, and may be partly determined by the market's interpretation or forecast of the business scene in the future. If there is a perception of declining business activity in the future, the risk averter segment will grow, and companies with stable earnings will be bid up in price. As a result of this market activity, given different perceptions by different investors, the slope of the central market will increase. The general demand for stability will be felt throughout the market, over time, as deeper discounts will be required to entice the risk taker into the lower end of the market, and more investors of the central market will take on aspects of the risk averter. Should the general feeling of increasing risk pervade in the market, all securities will be somewhat discounted over time, and the general level of the market, including the central market, will move downward.

Figure 10 - 2
MARKET VALUATION OF SOME LISTED UTILITIES

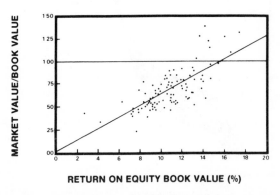

RETURN ON EQUITY BOOK VALUE (%)

Within that general market structure, there are many items that weigh heavily on the market evaluation. Each stock usually resides with a conceptual industry that has peculiar characteristics that in some way reflect on its value in the market. For example, in highly regulated fields such as communications, the required investments are particularly large, and the environment reasonably stable, and a particular level of return is allowed, under certain rules. Thus, prices are set by costs and required return to procure adequate capital. Interestingly, the efficiency of assets is seldom considered by the market. It may be that an efficiently operating public utility would have a smaller asset base than another comparable less efficient utility, have less stability in earnings, have less controllable costs and thus less upside potential, and thus have an earnings stream valued at less than the inefficient utility. Such a situation exists in the market, and it is not only allowed, but primarily caused by the regulatory body that controls the operations of that utility. The evaluation by the market is completely correct, in terms of financial evaluation of the return and risk of the assets. See Figure 10-2.

Figure 10 - 3
MARKET VALUATION OF ASSETS

A pleasing alternate is found in the processed foods industry. The margin here typically is less than two and a half percent of sales, and downside potential can be large. The market is willing to pay for efficiency and stability, as shown in Figure 10-3. There is a central market area, in which the general relationship of the market is reasonably consistent. There is a segment of risk aversion, in which the more efficient companies are desired and pursued by upward price bidding. There is the risk taker at the low end of the market, willing to buy the assets at some discount, assumably understanding the risk associated with those assets. In this example, then, efficiency of assets is a strong consideration in market valuation.

The general level of prices may be effected by dividend policy and growth rates. In times of uncertainty, investors typically want a higher dividend. In fact, for the market as a whole, reasonable dividend levels have become a prime requirement for market acceptance. At the same time, investors are looking for opportunities to "capitalize future earnings". A company with good growth opportunities will be a desirable company in a secure market position, and the management would find it profitable to use retained earnings as a capital source. This reinvested capital, if efficiently used, at some future time becomes worth some multiple, as valued by the market. There is, thus, an upper limit and a lower limit to what is a reasonable dividend level.

These levels themselves are not fixed, because they will change with the uncertainty of the market, just as it varies within industries. There is a general continuum from inadequate dividend payout, perhaps from lack of earnings, to overabsorption of earnings for internal use. Usually, the dividend policy will be determined by factors outside the market and internal to the firm.

Of course, to capitalize future earnings means to gain a tax break in the investment. This is a reasonably consistent factor in the market in the short run, as governmental revenue policy is not highly volatile. In the long run, it means that potential capital gains from reinvestment of earnings and growth can be valued more than current dividends. Certainly, taxes are rising for the average investor. Not only is inflation pushing most taxpayers into higher brackets of taxation without increase in purchasing power, but collection agencies such as the IRS are attempting, through administrative fiat, to increase tax rates, by deleting deductions. It seems that this consideration must become more important in the future.

135

The capitalization of future earnings often is accomplished outside the particular security being considered, by merger and acquisition. If a company with a P/E of 15 acquires a smaller company with a P/E of 5, the earnings of the high P/E company will appear to rise in the following year. It's the old game played strongly in the '60s, when the mania on the part of many company managements for playing the market made them forget insignificant things like efficiently operating assets. They merely acquired some new companies and were able to maintain the earnings, for a short time. The bubble did burst, but the game is still played, and from both ends. Fast growing companies are still a desirable commodity, as they probably always will be, and the fastest way to grow is through acquisition. Investors will often pay a premium for an agressive management that will use their market position (high P/E) to improve that particular security. The market may lose overall, but that particular security is stronger, and may better serve the investor.

The game can be played from the other end. If you hold a small company that has gained stability and reasonable earnings, and yet the market still will not recognize your accomplishments with what you consider an adequate P/E, it is possible to actively seek merger or acquisition by some large and more recognized firm. The result of success is a substantial increase in value, without much change in structure. The small company pursuing such a line may also be serving its investors, although the selection of that stock is lost to the market.

Some investors don't want to make up their own mind, and so they will buy what the institutional investors are buying in the market, regardless of price or internal value. The institutional investors are the pros, and they would know the best investment. This may be, but the funds have consistently underperformed the market averages. (Perhaps the investor should buy what the institutional investor is not buying.) The problem is that often the market as a whole overprices issues that have desirable characteristics, the same characteristics that drew the institutions to them. Thus, a recognized stock that has large holdings in the institutions is almost assured of being overpriced. This means that the return will be diminished for that security, even if growth and earnings are reasonable.

Buying that overpriced stock must rest on the bigger sucker hope. Earnings and growth will be inadequate to allow upward appreciation in line with more reasonably priced stocks, and the large holdings (demand) will be the only thing holding the price at its lofty levels. Should there be a shift in the stock and the institutions decide to move from that stock, the fundamental value cannot support it, and the stock price will go down.

Of course, the institutions are stuck in the market. They do not have the option of withdrawing from it, no matter how bad their future expectations may be (as discussed in Chapter 3). Should an investor follow the institutions into a stock, he may find out that the reasons for the investment by the institutions were completely contrary to his investment objectives. An institution might be taking a position in an issue for merely defensive reasons, knowing that the market is declining. An individual investor has the option of pulling out of the market at this point, and should do so. Following the institutions into an issue could cost a large amount of capital.

When he makes the decision to buy, an investor should also be making the decision to sell. The search may be for a stock that is underpriced, with the hope of taking a position in the issue within 10% of its market low. (Expecting to consistently buy at the low is not a feasable objective.) If you feel that the stock is underpriced, then you must have some idea of what a realistic price would be. That is the first step in looking for a sell point. It might be assumed that the realistic price was arrived at by evaluating the potential income stream, and measuring it in historical perspective of the stock, and its market evaluation. Then the stock could be related to the current or future market, and a potential future price arrived at. The volatility (Beta) of the stock will be a prime consideration in projecting a future price, in relation to the market.

What no investor can afford to do when valuing a stock is to think that the market is wrong. There are aberrations in the market, and certainly, an investor must search for them. More often than not, though, the market is right and the investor is wrong. Where the market is usually wrong is in overreacting to tomorrow's events. When a single stock is overpriced, it is usually in the company of many other overpriced stocks. There are minor imperfections visible in the market, but seldom can they be turned to the advantage of the individual investor. The decision to sell must be made knowing that today the market is valuing the security properly, but tomorrow, circumstances and projections will have changed, one way or another, and the valuation will have changed. Only the change is certain; the market seldom stands still in the long term.

In all of the relations mentioned above, there are leads and lags to their reflection in the market. Risk averters typically lead the market, hopping like scared jackrabbits to their "safe" investments at the first sign of trouble. The market in general is slower to react, and usually has a lag built into its short term movements, although in the long term it usually leads the business cycle. Investor confidence, the prime determinant in the slope and level of the market, is slow to change, although once it changes, reaction can become an avalanche.

When trying to determine future prices, it is possible to prepare a profile of potential prices, perhaps based on probability, or some similar estimating method. But don't sit down and start counting your money based on a paper method of price estimating. It is easy at this point to lose sight of the market action, and its attitude toward the stock you are considering. The risk that will be accepted at each price must be understood, and excessive risk must be guarded against. There is a way to do this, as we will now see.

Part III / The Particular Stock

Chapter 11

Skewness

A look at methods of the future for profitability now.

There is one thing about which we can be sure, and that is that the market will vacillate. Sometimes it is going up, and sometimes it is going down, but it seldom remains constant over any appreciable period of time. There are times when the market vacillates within only small limits, which, according to the technician, is a period of "consolidation". By definition, this period is a preparation for a move in one direction or the other.

It is not surprising that the market behaves as it does. It is a consolidation of numerous individual stocks, numerous industries, and the numerous economic and market effects on the many issues. Statistically, it might be expected that a total composed of so many small effects would be inherently unstable.

The purpose of the capital markets is to offer investors a medium of investment in which efficient business operations are rewarded with a commensurate return. In the market, this is seldom accomplished. There are the leads and lags that effect each individual stock that might be anticipated, the stocks being part of a much larger system. It is not surprising that stocks have a price influenced by anticipated business conditions and the business cycle, interest rates, political considerations, etc.

But even if the market risk is discounted, each stock vacillates from day to day, oftentimes without the event of seemingly important news. Some of this is due to the reasonably slow action of the market, in which long term changes take place over a long period of time, with built in lags to the accomplishment of price moves. There is an inertia in individual stocks that limit the range of change. In other times, there is a consolidation of opinion about a particular stock that groups the moves of individual investors into an avalanche of action. Such an action of so numerous a group of participants usually overreacts, once set in motion. When the price of a particular issue has an action beyond what might be expected from a particular event, there must be an adjustment over time back to a more reasonable valuation.

The real difficulty in the market, though, is finding that reasonable valuation. It seems that the market is unable to reach a consolidated opinion on what the real value of a security should be. As sophisticated as we may believe we are in business, the art of valuation is not particularly far advanced. The general consensus of the market has a strong effect on a final valuation, but the numerous factors mentioned above are difficult to properly weigh when valuing a particular security. Each analyst will weigh the factors differently, resulting in some variance in their final value.

That particular value must then be interpreted by each investor in terms of his own needs. He may weight the factors differently, and each issue may fit a different portion of his needs. A risk averter may see an individual issue differently and of a different value than the risk taker. The portfolio diversification of the investor may place a different need, and hence a different value, on each issue. Each investor will enter the market at a different time, vying for an issue at his price, or finding a particular price enticing him to sell.

On top of all this uncertainty, there is the acton of the specialist or market maker in each stock. For example, a security might be issued at a particular price, that price being the result of carefully considered opinions of the underwriters. It would not be unusual to see the stock up a few points by midday on the first day of trading. The same stock might be down a few points by the end of that trading day. The same kind of vacillations, though somewhat subdued, will continue throughout the life of that security. Certainly, some of that variance is due to the many forces acting on the market valuation of that issue. Other actions are often unexplained, and appear to be the arbitrary functioning of the specialist.

All of the factors act differently on a particular stock at a particular time. Of this we can be sure: the market, and each individual stock will continue to vacillate in price. To be an effective investor, or speculator, that fact must be accepted, and the market strategy and tactics of each individual investor must in some way deal with it. Variance in price is not all bad. If you own a stock, it would be thrilling to see the price rise, even though it was considered "fairly" valued when purchased. The most effective market approach would be one that enhanced the upward variations, and limited the downward price changes.

If we were to look at the historical annual highs and lows of a particular stock, there would be few that did not have some reasonably high variance within each year. In fact, if an investor could gain at least half of each year's variance, he would be certainly most pleased with the return on his portfolio, given the proper investments. Some of the variance would be in price declines, which could be gained only through short selling or the use of put options. While the gains can be limited in this approach to the market, or the risk high, it should always be a consideration in a well rounded program of investment.

Investors have always used some central measure for valuing a security. This has often been the mean (average) of price, earnings, or some other measure of performance of that security. In statistical terms, the mean is the first moment of a statistical distribution. In the last few decades, methods have been devised to include the second moment, the variance of an issue. In terms of price, this has meant measuring the variances of the individual issue in terms of the market as a whole. A highly volatile stock might vary with the market, but the price would change at a much higher percentage than would the market as a whole. This would be considered a risky stock, in terms of most stock market valuation theories. A less volatile stock might vary much less than the market as a whole, and thus be considered a conservative, and less risky stock. Since overall return allowed by the market is related to risk, with increasing returns associated with increasing risk, the more volatile stock would perhaps be assigned a lower P/E by the market action.

If the future actions of the market were perfectly symetrical at a particular time, such a valuation would be theoretically correct. However, there is seldom a time when, at least conceptually, it is not known that there is an upward or downward bias to the future actions of the market. This bias can be represented statistically by the third moment of a distribution, the skewness. If the market is generally considered to be biased toward higher prices, it would be best to invest in an issue that is "risky", and has high upward potential in relation to the market. If the bias of the market is toward lower prices, an investor could accept a defensive posture by investing in a less "risky" asset, so that downward movement in price would be minimized. Alternately, he could engage in short selling of a "risky" asset that would have high potential downward price movement, or simply stay out of the market. Certainly, at times when there is little bias to the market, prior to market turns, it would be wise not to participate in such a market. **A high degree of skewness is a prime requirement for participation in the market.**

The relation of a stock to the general market is most often shown by the Beta of a stock. A Beta of zero indicates that the stock variances are not affected by the market as a whole. A Beta of 1.00 would indicate that all the variances in the stock are explained by the variances of the market. When the bias of the market is upward, the confident investor would look for a stock with a Beta of 1.30+ perhaps. Of course, the Beta can only be measured historically to such precision, and a high Beta would be no guarantee that the stock would act similarly in the future. The changing character of the stock and the market valuation of those changes must always be considered.

At a particular time, it might be possible to prepare a probability profile for a particular stock, as shown in Figure 11-1. This profile is the result of fundamental analysis of the

Figure 11 - 1
PROBABILITY PROFILE

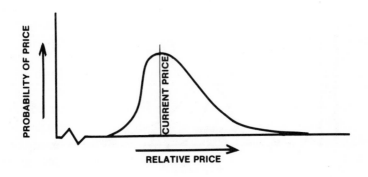

stock, general economic analysis, and market analysis, including technical analysis. It will contain, hopefully as little as possible, the intuitive feeling of the investor concerning future events. Note that the probability of a price decline is small in this example, and the amount of decline is a small percentage, compared to the upward bias. This would be an ideal time for investment, assuming the correctness of the profile, and would be the type found at the bottom of a market cycle. It is a reasonably riskless investment, even though standard measures of market "risk" might indicate that the risk was particularly high.

The risks represented in the profile can be generally classified under two headings, business risk and market risk. The business risk is derived from fundamental analysis and economic analysis, while the market risk is derived from technical and general market analysis, including considerations of levels of return and inflation. It is often wise to separate these two in a probability profile, because they can often be confused in the mind of the investor. Such a separation is shown in figure 11-2. In the case shown, note

Figure 11-2
STOCK PRICE SKEWNESS

(At A Particular Time)

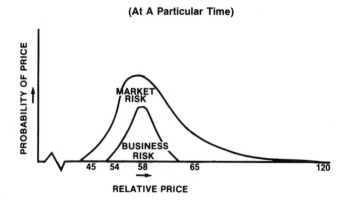

that the busines risk is reasonably symetrical, and that the range is quite small. The market risk is quite volatile, but skewed toward an investment decision. This is the kind of profile that might be found in a primary (blue chip) stock at the bottom of the market cycle. The market is leading the business cycle, and the stability of the company seems assured by its economic market position and the stability of its industry. However, the stock is underpriced by the overaction of the market, and a correction appears necessary, which will be amplified by a rising market within the timing scope of the profile.

A profile exists only at a certain time, and represents the possible price changes for a given time period. Note also that the market risk profile and business risk profile are determined from different sources. Some decision must be made as to which is dominant and to what degree. In a highly volatile stock (high Beta), the market will dominate, usually, but in certain stocks that are highly leveraged toward profit/loss, the business risk can dominate. In some more stable industries, such as utilities, they may be approximately equal in their potential effect on variability. Normally, it will be found that the market risk dominates the valuation of an industrial stock.

That valuation division between the two risks could be strongly affected by the level of market valuation of that stock. If the stock is valued with a relatively low P/E, and resides in the market segment of speculators, the market may forgive business risk. A company in this market segment might show a quarterly loss, without strong effect on the price, as long as the potential of future profits was not adversly changed. A stock considered an appropriate investment by risk averters, assigned a relatively high P/E by the market would not be so easily forgiven. The business risk can thus become dominant in the risk averter segment of the market, while the market risk would be a stronger consideration in the risk taker segment. This is because the risk of loss has already been discounted by the risk taker market, and high variability of returns is acceptable to those investors.

Those factors and the place assigned to a stock by the market must always be considered when preparing a profile. It will also determine what kind of profile is acceptable to the particular investor. For example, note in Figure 11-3A, that

Figure 11 - 3
TYPES OF SKEWNESS IN STOCK PRICES

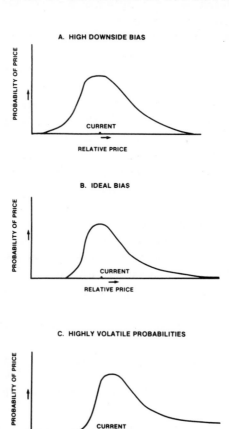

A. HIGH DOWNSIDE BIAS

B. IDEAL BIAS

C. HIGHLY VOLATILE PROBABILITIES

there is little bias upward. Such a profile would not be acceptable to any investor, whether he be a risk taker or risk averter. Of course, no investor wants to lose money in the market, and the ideal profile would be as shown in Figure 113B, similar to the skewness previously considered. Too much of a good thing can be questionable, though, and a profile such as shown in Figure 11-3C may indicate a highly volatile situation that a risk averter would best avoid. In the first place, such a profile probably results from investor hopes, rather than accurate evaluation of the current market or business risks. Such a profile is unlikely except through insider information, and then it is very short lived. If it exists, it probably depends on some event, which, even though seemingly assured, has its own risks. It is not a situation for the risk averter.

There are two ways in which the ideas of skewness and bias should be used by the individual investor. First, they should be used conceptually to view the position of the market currently, and how it might act in the future. This might be in the form of preparing a probability profile for the general market, using an accepted average measure, such as the Dow, S&P 500, NYSE composite, etc. Many market analysts do exactly this, when attempting to determine that "the Dow will peak at 1050", for example.

More importantly, the individual investor must gain a comprehensive understanding of valuation by the market, and this tool will allow him to think in terms of bias of the market, rather than in a symetrical variability, as he might have learned from current practice in market valuation techniques. The market is never stable, and all successful investors need to know is which way it will vacillate in a given time frame.

The same kind of thinking and evaluation, applied to the particular issue under consideration, may give some comprehension as to where that issue fits into the market. If it is leading the market, the timing is different than if the stock lags the general market action. If it is a risk averter stock, does the particular firm have characteristics that might be unacceptable to this segment of the market, given changing economic conditions? A loss of position for a risk averter stock has a disasterous effect on price. The high P/E simply melts away, taking with it the investor's capital.

The second way of using these ideas is in detailed analysis of the company. Operational analysis of the company will be required to properly prepare the business risk portion of the profile, and the characteristics discovered should add some comprehension of where the company stands in its industry and marketplace. The position of the company is constantly changing, and the direction of change is of great importance. If a company is moving toward its efficient operating point as it shifts its position in the marketplace, the upward bias to business risk will eventually be appreciated by the market. Companies being forced away from their efficient operating point will eventually lose some of their standing in the market.

However the profile is used, it has only one purpose, and that is risk minimization. In a volatile market, the investor must, above all, protect his capital. If such a tool can also be turned to the advantage of the investor in increasing his capital as well, it is valid to do so. This second objective, capital appreciation, is always subsidiary to the first objective, capital maintenance.

Part IV

Planning For A Return

For The Long Term

Chapter 12

Planning for a return.

Bulls and bears can make money,
pigs rarely do.

It is imperative that an investor have a definitive plan to guide his investing activities. Ask the average investor in the market what his purpose is and he will probably respond, "to make money". That leaves too many unanswered questions, primarily how and how much. Greed is not a successful motivation for investing, and it usually is the downfall when allowed to control. The old saying in the market is, "A bull or bear can make money, but a pig rarely can".

In the market, there is a general relationship between risk and return. To obtain a higher return, an investor must assume higher risk. In the central market, this relationship is reasonably consistent. At the extremes, the return is rarely adequate, as an average, to compensate the investor. You can't "beat the market" consistently, but you can allow the market to work for you in obtaining your objectives. Included in those objectives must be a sustainable return, or actions are merely a one time speculative fling. It may be acceptable to include in your objectives probable and possible appreciation of market value, but good investment practice precludes dreams of little substance. There are examples in the past of spectacular returns, and they will occur in the future, probably. But the mood of the market is changing, and most such gains were the result of luck as much as anything. Even in hindsight, few analysts (of the sane ones) can explain adequately most large price rises in individual issues. At the very least, the probabilities are against the investor's attempting to play that game.

Above all in importance is that an investment have strong fundamental value. This means that the business risk must be minimized by efficiently operating assets, and that the market risk must be minimized by a reasonable return level. A steady profits stream in a solid industry representing a return of 20% on market value (a P/E of 5) has little downside risk. A strong growth stock selling at a P/E of 12, purchased in timing with good potential for strong continued growth, will soon improve your market capital. This is probably a reasonable range for investing in today's market environment, sticking to the central market, and shunning the speculative extremes. These buys can be found, by allowing the emotional control of the market to overreact, and maintaining the conceputal stance that allows you to recognize the values when they appear.

But strong earnings are not adequate in themselves. The mood of the market is changing, and our financial system grows more precipitous with passing time. The credit crunches of '66, '69, and '74 were real enough, and governmental fiscal irresponsibility and rising inflation hardly bode well for the '79 money markets. It is the capital structure, measured by the adequacy for liquidity, that will become more important in the future. The past practice of adding dividends and growth to get a return may be inadequate in the future. The opportunities that occur in the economy may only be available to the firm that possesses adequate liquidity to pursue them. The vacillations of the money markets appear to be increasingly severe. The only protection an investor has may be fundamental value in an issue, in the Balance Sheet as well as the P&L.

Planning for a return involves a plan to sell, in existence at the time the decision is made to buy. This involves knowing the strengths and weaknesses of the individual issue, the characteristics of the relationship of the industry to the general economy, market perception of the individual issue, and potential changes in that perception. An estimate of future value does not have to be precise, and probably cannot be so, but the general direction in which changing characteristics will carry the issue must be understood. That is, in essence, the decision to buy.

It is completely possible to outperform the market through the simple strategy of avoiding the large losers. These are the companies that are either overpriced, or lack the fundamental value of efficient operation. Anyone who bought Eastman Kodak in the mid '70s at a P/E of 35 failed to recognize that the company, though stable, was reaching maturity, and that the mood of the market was changing from the growth craze of the '60s. Most of the overpriced "growth" issues have lost money for their investors.

There was also the example of a small company selling at 7, with a P/E of about 50 that seemed to have exceptional opportunity for major technical breakthroughs. It was being strongly supported by a brokerage firm, and so had excessive buying pressure. The firm has done well, increasing earnings by eight times over the past three years. It was too long a time for investors to wait, and the stock now sells at 5. It was too obviously overpriced, but it may now be a good buy. These firms were at the extremes of the market. One was the risk averter, who was actually taking a very large risk in the overpriced issues. The other was the speculator who was betting on an improbable growth rate. Fairy tales do happen, but the odds against it are astronomical.

Some recent studies indicate that the average return yielded to the investor is about 12% per year. An investor could have done much better or much worse than that, depending on when he got into and out of the market, and on the gains and lapses of the individual issues. Let's say that about 7% of that return was paid out, on an average. If we deduct transfer costs (commissions, etc.) and taxes at the individual tax rates, and then adjust for a 6% inflation, it is likely that the investor has lost purchasing power, without the capital appreciation. There may have been a net loss in capital, by assuming a stable market level. That's the status of the market: that an investor can only profit from the market through capital appreciation. Some of that is the result of poor tax policies, and some of it is the speculative nature of the market at this point of time. The lesson should be obvious enough: downside risk to capital must be minimized above all else. Upside potential will then be enhanced, so that we may gain at least some of the appreciation required to maintain the purchasing power of our capital base.

If we select stocks for fundamental value, and search out those with upside potential in market value, that potential can be enhanced with the use of the market segments. The two tier market that we experienced in '77 was merely a primary decline, while the tertiary stocks continued their advance. It was to be expected, and is reasonably explained by an understanding of the market segments. What that indicated is that stocks must be selected not only for their level in the market but for their stance in the depth of the market. It can be answered by the typical progression of an investor searching for better priced stocks with improved probability of return. It is unlikely that the investor will switch from a blue chip to a dog. The emotional constitution of all but the most extreme trader would be adverse to such a drastic change. The change in impetus of market depth comes slowly, over time, with a smoothness that results only from combining the numerous and carefully considered discrete decisions of the many investors. Considered in each of those decisions are the fundamentals of the firm and how it can react to a changing economy, as well as the capability of management to act in a specific environment. For certain types of firms and managements, there is a good time as well as a bad in the economic cycle, and this helps to determine the segment to which a firm belongs. After all, in the long run, it is smart management, not accounting conventions that determine price.

The theory in use of these segments would tell us to buy late and sell late as shown in Figure 12-1. The idea is that an investor should not buy in a declining market, and in fact to sell early might cut potential gains short. If, in fact, you buy fundamental value, it may be wise to buy early, knowing that the fundamental value of the issue will protect you on the downside. A wise investor may sell early, recognizing that excessive multiples are increasing the downside risk. In

Figure 12 - 1
USE OF TRENDS IN APPROACH TO MARKET

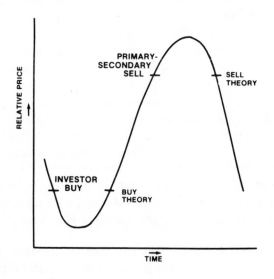

exchange for that security, some return potential may be given up, but the investor's capital is freed to participate in the next segment of the market. The important thing is not to risk the capital base by exposing it to excessive risk while hoping for some windfall. That's speculating at the fringes of the market, and never pays an adequate average return for the risk assumed.

One possible approach to the use of the market segments in an investment plan is shown in Table 12-1. The Table shows a possible allocation of funds to a portfolio, with each horizontal line totaling 100 percent. Note that the funds supporting this portfolio are entirely capital funds. They exclude emergency funds that should be held liquid (typically placed at six months living expenses), funds that must be held for other reasons, such as family health, and funds in a private firm, or used to secure a position, investment in personal assets such as a house, etc. The timing of the various investments are only approximate, for the relation of the interest rate cycle to the economy varies, for example, and we have already noted the reducing lead of the market on the economy. Even that long term trend is subject to change or variation. On the rising market, four major moves are identified: primary, secondary, and tertiary rising segments, and the primary/secondary reversal. The secondary/tertiary reversal is usually too ill defined to be of investment value, though it can be a trading tactic to the aggresive and knowledgable investor. In the historically shorter declining market, the secondary and tertiary segments often run together as general market moves. The continuum still exists in relating individual stocks to the general progression of depth in a major trend. It is still a strong indicator of timing, but is seldom reflected in definitive fashion in the general market averages. The tertiary decline turns into the primary rise, and it starts all over again.

It has been assumed that any residual funds would be invested in a short term money market vehicle, and this goes from a zero low to a high of 70% of the portfolio. Our major

Table 12 - 1
THE INVESTMENT CYCLE

Portfolio Percentages	Liquid Funds	Stocks	Bonds, Utilities, Regulated Companies	Warrants, Convertibles, Options	Bullion	Real Estate
Rising						
Primary		70	20	10		
Reversal	70	20 SHORT	10			
Secondary		70	20			10
Tertiary	10	50			20	20
Declining						
Primary	40	20 SHORT		(PUTS)	20	20
Reversal	60	10			10	20
Secondary/Tertiary	50	20 SHORT		(PUTS)	10	20
Determinant:	Residual	Market Cycle	Long Term Interest	Market Cycle	Inflation	Housing Cycle

159

vehicle is common stocks, and they go from 20% short to a high of 70% of the portfolio. The primary rise is the strongest move of a typical cycle, and so stock investment is at a maximum in this phase. That 70% might be broken down as 20% local stocks (geographical proximity), 20% in your specialty industry (technical proximity), 10% in more speculative issues (depending on your personal ability in stock selection and emotional control), and 20% in national issues.

Investments in bonds, utilities, and regulated companies are primarily controlled by the interest cycle, and this also typically leads the business cycle, and so lags even more the market cycle. During the secondary rise, when higher rates are typically developing , it may be approriate to purchase issues that have been supressed in price. Often times this yeilds such a good return that investors will retain the issues over the long term even though they appreciate in price. With the current changing mood of the market, and an increasing rate of inflation, this is not recommended. With increasing rates being demanded by the market, it is better to use the shorter term vacillations around that rising trend to your advantage, while searching out better investment vehicles over the longer term.

Options are flyers. You might gamble a thousand with the hopes of recovering up to a few hundred times your investment. For the most part, options serve a useful function in allowing an investor to protect his investment for a small insurance fee, just as currency futures protect the profit of an importer or exporter, or commodity futures protect the raw materials industrial user. With the exceptional leverage available, it may be acceptable for the knowledgable investor to participate in carefully selected issues through options as a speculation. Understand that such a move is a highly speculative one, with little real opportunity to make a significant return, and high probability of losing the entire investment. Other situations besides hedges, such as straddles and combinations are of little value to the non-trader. Once in a while an effective position appears, but usually the return profile is inadequate to compensate for the risk.

Options can be sold late in the upward move of a market segment by an investor who holds the stock long. The investor who sells such a call thereby increases the current return from the stock. He trades a definite return (the call proceeds) in exchange for the possibility of a much higher return (capital appreciation), which he relinquishes in the call.

Bullion, such as silver and gold, is seldom profitable because of the storage costs. There are times when it will tend to rise, particularly in conjunction with the increasing pessimism of a declining market. It seems reasonable to expect gold at $250/ounce and silver at $8/ounce prior to 1982. Depending on the severity of the current inflation cycle, it could go higher. That's not really a very good return over that period of time, and it is one that could be eaten up by maintenance costs. I would limit investment in precious metals to what can be personally stored and protected. The real return might be an improved composure and relaxation in times when the dollar constantly loses huge chunks of value.

A real estate column is not a reference to a second home in the mountains. It refers generally to ownership of real assets, similar to bullion, but capable of producing a return. This might be found in certain real estate operating stocks. It most certainly does not refer to the mortgage (non-equity) operations. Using real estate as the example, it should be noted that these stocks must be selected with great care. Certain geographical areas have grossly overpriced real estate, while other areas have lagged the price increases of inflation. The latter represent the fundamental values, a reasonable relation to replacement cost (after considering reasonable depreciation) in real estate. The cycle of these physical assets typically lags the inflation and interst rate cycles. In housing, the activity level lags the business cycle by only a few months, but price increases may take as long as two years to reach the far corners of the market.

That particular portfolio flow is what might be recommended for a somewhat agressive investor. The objective might still be primarily capital maintenance, but certain risks are proposed, offering adequate return to compensate, that a more conservative investor would not wish to take. A retired individual who did not need the increased income would perhaps adopt the more conservative approach, while a young man in his thirties with good earning power might feel it was too tame a program for him. It is presented as an agressive portfolio beyond which returns are inadequate to compensate for the increasing risk. But that is an individual decision and judgement.

There are numerous levels of growth that might be pursued, but it is a statistical truth that the higher the growth, the shorter the term over which it can be sustained. The probabilities of its occurance are also decreased. A particular breakthrough, market position, or changing need might allow a firm to increased profits by 5 times in a few years. Such a move in a "boom" company is usually unpredictable, and it is only the investor who is very near the situation who will have an opportunity to see the situation. Of these few, only a very small number will be able to see the forest for the trees. It is not really a situation an investor can successfully pursue.

The cyclical stocks, those with a high Beta, might improve profits as much as double with the changing business cycle, if the stock is in a position of high leverage. That would typically occur over a two year period average. That is probably the highest stable profit situation available for study by the investor. The long term growth stocks might produce an average 15% increase in earnings over an extended period of time. That is about a doubling every five years. This typically suits the conservative investor, and if purchased at fundamental value in the market, is a very profitable investment. The income stocks produce about a 7% to 8% normal growth in profits annually, with a doubling about every 9 or 10 years. These stocks have a place in a portfolio, but proper alternatives with minimum risk preclude them from constituting a major portion of a reasonable portfolio.

It might be of value to speculate on the potential returns on a typical portfolio throughout the market cycle. Some possible values are shown in Table 12-2, broken down by the major market segment moves, and cumulated over the typical cycle. Returns are broken down into dividends (current) and capital gains (future potential). The dividends can be reasonably assured at the time of purchase, but note that the 7.5% average annual return would not even cover the inflation premium in today's market, after deducting transaction costs and a nominal tax rate. The capital gains, or some portion of them, will result from accurate stock

Table 12 - 2
POSSIBLE RETURNS IN A MARKET CYCLE

	Period (Years)	Dividends (%)	Cumulative (%)	Capital Gains (%)	Cumulative (%)	Total Return (%)
Primary Stocks	1	6	6	25	25	31
Secondary Stocks	¾	8	12	35	69	87
Tertiary Stocks	¾	5	17	50	153	190
Cash	½	8	21		153	213
Bonds	1	10	33	20	204	307
	4					
Average Annual Rate		7.5		32		42

selection in fundamental value and timing. If a proper conceptual approach to investing can be maintained, the potential returns can be highly profitable. Even using this conservative portfolio, the total return is over 300% (that is, the initial investment appreciates to 400%). There is at least as much upside potential to this portfolio as there is downside potential, so that the total return can be highly variable from that shown. The return level will depend primarily on the ability to select fundamental value in conjunction with market position.

There is no unique formula that will yield overnight riches in the market. It is a reasonable approach that can yield adequate and consistent returns, allowing the investor to be a part of the market, with some potential for additional returns, while using the market variances. This approach requires a knowledge of the changing conditions of the market, and a conceptual recognition of its level at any time. Investing in the market is becoming more difficult, with lesser chance for gain, and higher risk which results from weaknesses of the financial system. The coming requirement will be a conservative capital structure. Firms meeting this requirement will be able to maintain liquidity in difficult times. They may thus take advantage of opportunities as these opportunities present themselves.

Summary

The stock market is a capital market and, as such, has as its primary function the channeling of capital funds into the economy. Capital funds are by nature long term funds, and therefore the nature of the stock would apropriately be long therefore the nature of the stock would appropriately be long term. To be effective in providing its funtion of channeling of funds, a certain degree of liquidity is necessary. Unfortunately, the successes of the market and its associated economic functions have attracted an excess of funds. The nature of the stock market has tended toward short term. The excess volatility of the market has often caused a loss of proper valuation levels, and vacillations have resulted which subordinate the proper function of the market. The simple action of placing funds into the flow of the market is no longer investing. Capital values are lost, not to the business risk of the economic functions, but to the market risk of inappropriate valuations. The market has assumed the short term characteristics of a money market, and placing funds in the market has become an act of speculation.

There are underlying values that exist in the market at a time, and they can offer the investor the potential that might be found in a more appropriately functioning capital market. The true (conservative) investor can follow certain techniques that allow him to place funds in an economic venture, and enjoy the successes of the enterprise.

The source of power is sometimes only adequate information, of an accurate and timely nature. The width of the market makes it difficult to maintain current information on any large portion of it. It is better to be well informed about one stock, than to have general information about the entire market. One method for the individual to obtain the information necessary to him is to select areas of concentration with which he can maintain direct contact. Physical or geographical proximity is one area that the individual can effectively follow, through news media and local business contacts. An individual can also follow the stocks of his technical specialty in business, thereby maintaining daily contact and gaining a source of direct information in detail.

The stocks must then be carefully selected for fundamental value. There are three risks that must be guarded against through use of this fundamental value. The first is the most important, for it has been neglected somewhat successfully over the past few decades. The changing character of the financial structure will no longer allow that. That risk is financial risk, the loss of liquidity, and it is controlled by Balance Sheet management. The second risk is the business risk, embodied in the operation of the economic enterprise. It is the functioning of the assets of the firm. If they are efficient, the P&L can show sustained profitability. The third risk is the market risk, and it is much larger than is appropriate for a capital market. It is controlled by the investor through proper pricing, refusing to accept issues that carry a price above its basic economic value in providing a consistent return.

Minimizing these three risks means minimizing the downside potential in price, lack of profitability, and illiquidity. In the technical theory of the market, variance in any direction is considered risk. The successful investor will guard against downside risk, and yet happily greet the assumable risk of upside potential. In this way the vacillations of the short term market are made to work for the investor. In fact, it is necessary to include capital appreciation in the total return to maintain an adequate profit in today's market.

To minimize the market risk, the investor must understand the vacillations of the market, and comprehend its direction. The direction may be pointed out by the moods of the market. They are long term phenomena that slowly move the level of the market, change its priorities, and effect the importance of its components. In the medium term, there is a strong market cycle that represents a continual redevelopment of the market, through the probing of

167

investors for better investments. A depth to the market is thus developed as the market becomes stronger. It improves the selection of issues, but also controls the timing of the investor into particular types of issues. The general progression is from the large and stable issues, sought by the risk averter, to the smaller and more volatile issues, sought by the risk taker. It is a showing of confidence by the market participants as it develops its strength.

But once set in motion, the market seldom knows where to stop. From a base of economic valuation, the market rides on emotion, until the values of issues are unrealistic. There has been an overreaction to the expected continuance in economic expansion. The movement is difficult to stop, but once motionless, the lack of values becomes dominant, and a reversal is eminent. The market thus goes on its way, but it offers recurring opportunities to invest in a particular type of issue, though under differing conditions each time.

There are many ways to invest in the market, and the continuum of stocks is beyond the needs of any investor. Some investors may wish to be agressive, and accept additional risk in exchange for the opportunity of increased return. Others may wish to reduce the risk, and are willing to accept a reduced return. Both serve a useful function in the market. It is necessary that each investor determine for himself what he expects from the market. Appropriate long term planning is essential for the success of the individual investor.

The method shown here is not a formula for a get rich quick scheme. Any method so purported would be a fraud. What is presented are some guidelines for successful investing in a speculative market. It is a method of providing more than a reasonable return, while assuming minimum risk to the capital base. This method is more of an admonition: to only accept investment values in a volatile market. It should assure the investor that these values are there and assist him in finding them. If the investor searches for them, while maintaining a conceptual view of the market and its directions, he will be a successful investor.

Additional copies of this book may be obtained
for $8.95 (paperback) or $12.95 (hardcover) from:

Concept Publishing
Box 203
York, New York 14592

Write for special discounts.

Concept Publishing is interested in any publications that advance
the knowledge of management, or deal with conceptual matters,
in extending knowledge of the discipline.

LONG TERM INVESTING

An investment service that includes:

1. A monthly letter of long term timing, investing services, and economic development.

2. Special Investment Advisories recommending specific buys and sells, prepared as required by timing, approximately once per month.

3. Review of special investment situations on subscriber request, twice a year.

4. A copy of *For The Long Term.*

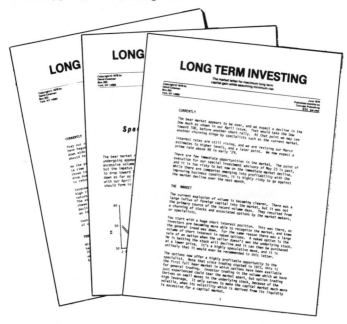

Following the principles of this book, Concept Publishing prepares an investment service covering the market and development level, market structure changes, industry studies, economic status, and specific stock recommendations.

Subscriptions are limited to 200.
A sample copy may be obtained by writing:
Concept Publishing
Box 203
York, New York 14592

Subscriptions are $70.00 per year.
(Credit for the price of the book will be given if a copy is already owned.)

MAJOR MARKET TURNS

Monthly Letter, October 1976:

"Plan for a market exit between March '77 (for primary stocks) and June '77 (for tertiary stocks)."

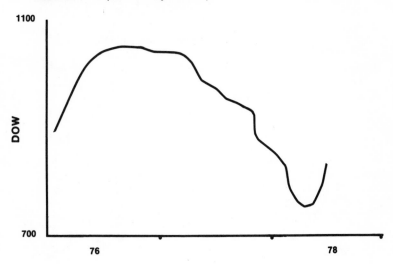

SHORT TERM,
HIGH PROFIT SPECULATION

Special Investment Advisory, June 23, 1978:

"We expect the Dow to drop toward 700 ... and ... Kodak stock to move toward 50 ... Buy 60 July puts with the stock above 57 for a sell with the stock at 52."

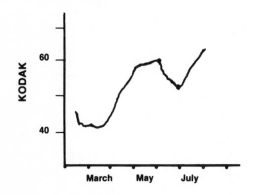